ROYAL MAIL

Frontispiece]

TOP: A contemporary illustration showing the dress of a foot Post in the early 17th Century. BOTTOM: The cover of an Elizabethan letter showing the " Post Haste " orders and the gallows warning. The letter probably concerned defence matters for Kent at the time of the Armada.

ROYAL MAIL

THE STORY OF THE POSTS IN ENGLAND FROM THE TIME OF EDWARD IV TH TO THE PRESENT DAY

F. GEORGE KAY

FELLOW OF THE ROYAL SOCIETY OF ARTS

SALISBURY SQUARE LONDON

Made and printed in Great Britain by
THE CENTRAL PRESS
ABERDEEN

CONTENTS

v

ILLUSTRATIONS

*The illustration used for the end papers of this book, showing a
north-east view of the New General Post Office in the early 19th
Century, is reproduced by permission from the engraving by
H. Pyall, in the Headquarters Building, G.P.O., St. Martin's-le-
Grand, London*

To the men and women of the postal services
whose work enhances the welfare and happiness
of mankind

1

THE ROYAL MAIL BEGINS

O F the many contributions of service to modern civilisation which Britain can be proud to record there can be few of such unassailable and universal benefit as the postal system. It is true that Posts were organised in Europe long before couriers bearing the Royal Arms of England galloped northwards on the King's business more than four and a half centuries ago. But it was the Royal Mail which first became a right for all instead of a privilege of the few. The plans of a succession of bold and imaginative men brought a cheap and efficient service which became at first the envy of, and later the example for, other countries. The tradition that the mail is sacred, that its expedition on its journeyings precedes almost every other consideration, stems from this country. It is a remarkable fact in the troubled times in which we live that the world postal organisation is the nearest approach to complete international understanding and co-operation that can be found. The ability of any person in the world to send a letter to another, wherever he may be, is regarded as a natural thing. No better testimonial could be required as to the sound basis on which the posts were built from the very beginnings of a rudimentary system of fifteenth-century England until the present time with the peoples of the world " held together by a postage stamp ".

Couriers carrying Royal messages, with power to requisition horses and guides, were operating from the earliest times. The system was known as " post through " or " through post ". In times of emergency an arrangement whereby specially mounted messengers carried " pacquets " in relays goes back to these days, but the first definite mention of it is found at the time of war between England and Scotland when Edward IV appointed a single horseman for every twenty miles to carry his orders and to bring him news from the north. Considering the state of the roads at that time, it was a remarkably efficient service. A letter was carried 200 miles in two days. The horsemen were strictly ordered not to exceed their twenty miles to keep up maximum speed. Two years later, in 1484, with Richard III on the throne, the same system was started to provide warning of the expected landing of Henry of Richmond, who after the victory of Bosworth, ascended the throne of England.

Even from those early days the rights of the Posts took precedence over ordinary communications and travel. The couriers could requisition horses wherever they wished, and so far as can be discovered they paid for them practically what they chose. The local authorities were compelled to grant every facility to the King's Mail, and it is likely that even then the cry " Post haste! " was heard in the yards of inns and market squares as the messenger galloped in. Instantly all was activity: the impatient official would examine the horses in the stables with an expert eye and select the one he preferred. Maybe it was the palfrey of the local priest or prosperous merchant; perhaps only a mud-bespattered pony of a visiting farmer was available. But he took the best he could find and went on his way. No one could complain: this was the King's business, and the leather pouch strapped to his waist was the Royal Mail.

Such Posts were not permanent. The routes were moved according to the exigencies of the Wars of the Roses as the rival houses of York and Lancaster fought for the throne. There must have been a guiding brain to organise these sudden and urgent changes in the routes. Whoever was responsible to the King for their efficiency has not been recorded, so that the name of the first Postmaster-General cannot be honoured as it deserves.

Probably officials of the court and officers of the Army made use of this Royal Post if occasion arose, but it was certainly not available to anyone except to intimates of the King. This applied to the King's Post, but in London the growing commercial power of the capital had created a considerable service of carriers whose horse-drawn wagons groaned along the remains of the Roman roads during the dry months of summer. These carriers were especially busy in the prosperous Eastern Counties, where the great weaving industries were centred, and were left comparatively unscathed by the military operations of civil war, which ranged from Barnet to Northampton, from Tewkesbury to Wakefield.

Naturally, these carriers would take messages for a fee, and undoubtedly a widespread but haphazard postal service grew up in this way.

It was slow and irregular, because wagoners rarely risked travelling alone. They travelled in long trains for mutual protection. The risks were certainly not imaginary. Robbery and death were the lot of those who had to travel the roads of England at that time if they did not have the means to resist. The packhorses and the wagoners had many guard dogs—the fox-hounds of to-day—and armed men riding ahead and behind. The perils of the road did not come only from outlaws and criminals. In the Midlands and the North barons were often as wicked as folklore paints them. Bands of armed men would replenish the family coffers by robbery of travellers or holding them to ransom. Poorer people would simply be rounded up and held as serfs to work on the land. Only the holy men on pilgrimages were safe from these depredations.

Only in the summer or for reasons of urgency did the wagoners travel by night. Their journey was based on the literal meaning of the phrase, " a day's travel ". Indeed, it was in many parts illegal to move by night. Bells were rung in the towns to warn travellers that the gates would soon be shut, and many churches maintained beacons on their towers to help the traveller caught on the road. There were no milestones (the Roman examples now to be seen have all been dug out and renovated since those times) and no signposts. Anyone out at night who missed the vague track of the road might find himself up to the shoulders in water or plunging down a fifty-foot cliff. It is no wonder that the merchants were quite content with twelve miles in a day, and we may admire the Royal messengers who could far exceed this by risking travel by night, when even the protection of their Royal badge must have been slight among the outlaws who infested the deeply wooded England of the fifteenth century.

Simultaneously there was a privileged message service running between the monasteries and religious establishments which had lands and buildings widely separated. They were concerned with their own affairs, but were widespread, reaching to most parts of Europe. Ordinary folk could not make use of them, and their sole means of communication were through the wagoner. It must be remembered that no peasant or labourer, even a freeman, could travel without a permit on pain of imprisonment. The sheriff could issue this passport, but very rarely did, even for pilgrimages. If such people wished to acquaint relations about some family matter, the wagon post was the only available method. The evidence of the way these unofficial posts worked comes mostly from the Paston letters, written between 1432 and 1509 by a Norfolk family. Some of them went a considerable distance, and from the mere fact that they have been handed down to us it is evident that they were safely delivered, despite the vague addresses. Even to-day the G.P.O. could justifiably be proud if it carried to its destination a letter addressed like this: " To Thomas Grene, goodman of the George, by Powles Wharffe, or hys wyff, to send to Sir John Paston, whereso evere he be, at Caleys, London or other placeys." Caleys is, of course, Calais, so it is evident that the Norwich carriers were quite ready to accept a message even if it had to go across the sea to England's last possession in France.

By the end of the fifteenth century, England had the Royal Mail system, acting only when occasion arose, the monastic posts, and the side-line services of the carriers. When Henry VIII came to the throne in 1509, he must have noted the growing volume of private correspondence with some misgivings. Treasonable plots could be thwarted when those known to be disaffected travelled to some meeting-place in person. This disaffection, hatched by means of correspondence, possibly even with potential enemies abroad, would simply not be known until it was too late. Probably this was one reason why a postal service controlled by the Crown was then planned; another was that it clearly provided a most useful source of revenue in days when the King was invariably hard put to it to obtain the finance he needed.

Very soon after he ascended the throne, Henry appointed a Master of the King's Posts. The first one whose name is known was Brian Tuke, who had been appointed Clerk of the Signet at the Coronation, and was known officially as the Postmaster seven years later. Brian Tuke was the son of Richard Tuke, a member of the household of the Duke of Norfolk. The small boy received an education which was only possible for children who lived in the manors of the aristocracy, and through the influence of his father's employer Brian obtained employment as King Henry VII's Bailiff at Sandwich at a wage of 12d. per day (about 15s. in to-day's values). A year later Henry VII died and Henry VIII came to the throne. He was a young man of eighteen, and was naturally attracted to the young official much the same age as himself. Taken into the King's personal retinue, Brian Tuke was set on the ladder of a comfortable livelihood and possible fame, though he would probably have been amazed that the office of Postmaster was destined to be the means of achieving them both.

By 1510 Brian Tuke was Clerk of the Council at Calais, and in this post he was able to see some of the advantages of an official postal service to handle the considerable flow of commercial and official business which flowed across the Channel between Dover and England's outpost on the continent of Europe.

The way he handled the King's business in France came to the notice of the great Cardinal Wolsey, with the result that Brian Tuke was recalled and appointed secretary to the Chancellor, receiving a knighthood at the same time. The young secretary's job was to see that both his master's correspondence and that of his King went speedily and safely to the four corners of the realm. The somewhat haphazard Posts which then existed enabled the principal routes to be covered. In 1513 when invasion from Europe threatened, it was by the Posts that all along the coast the inhabitants were warned to brew beer and make biscuits in readiness for the sailors and soldiers who would be stationed at the seaports. Tuke could send letters to Exeter by a series of nine horsemen, and the Post to Dover was ready to convey all the messages which sped between England and France in preparation for the meeting between Henry of England and Francis of France at the Field of the Cloth of Gold, near Calais.

The size of the Posts after Sir Brian Tuke took charge was considerable. As early as 1513 the amount granted to Tuke to pay for the men and horses on the northern route was £578 4s. 3d., and as 12d. per day was a typical fee for an individual courier, the number employed and the amount of work they had to do must have been fairly large.

Tuke must have been a harassed man. In his position as Clerk of the Signet, he was the chief letter-writer of the Government; more than that, he was responsible for seeing that the letters reached their destination. The vital business with Europe was, according to the officials at Calais and in the foreign courts, jeopardised by delays, and these were laid at the door of Tuke. Gradually, in typical English fashion, the work he was doing to put the Posts right was recognised by the creation of a position for the job long after he had been devoting most of his time to it.

For some years he carried on with the situation, but in 1533 (Wolsey had died in 1530) he wrote a letter to Sir Thomas Cromwell, in which he met the complaints and showed the problems he was up against. This letter provides a vivid description of the Posts of Tudor times. From its contents, it is shown that the postal service to the North was the least blameworthy, and that the London-Dover service compared badly with that in France because there were hackney horses only between Gravesend and Dover. Elsewhere, at each stage the local authorities, with no warning that a Post was coming through, were confronted with the problem of finding a mount quickly, possibly even in the night. " The constables many tymes be fayn to take horses out of plowes and cartes, wherein ", says Tuke with a trace of sarcasm, " can be no extreme diligence." The difficulties of running an efficient service with the miserable budget allowed with typical Tudor parsimony, when the King's Mail had to lumber a stage further with the postman mounted on a heavy plough horse, was indeed a sorry picture and an unenviable burden for the Master of the Posts.

There is also evidence in this letter that the prevalent custom of blaming the Post Office for one's own delays or omissions of correspondence was already in fashion. According to Tuke, writers dated their letters a day or two earlier than they were actually written; requests to " my Lord of Northumberland " to mark the time and date of despatch on the back were continually made, but seldom observed, while this gentleman failed to co-operate with other officials in the North by sending his letters at the same time of the day as they did. Consequently, the unfortunate Posts would take a letter from the Earl of Northumberland in the morning, return to find one waiting despatch from Lord Dacre, and in the evening have to set out a third time with yet another from Sir George Lawson. All had, of course, to be sent off immediately, no matter how weary horseman and horse, the triple journey continuing at every stage right down to London.

Despite all these early troubles, England established a postal service during Sir Brian Tuke's career which became a permanent feature of national life. The term " post haste " was already in the language as a description of the speediest journey possible, and many travellers desirous of getting from one town to another quickly would ride post—that is, they would adopt the system of changing horses every twenty miles and probably employ a postboy to show them the route. The couriers, since they were appointed by Royal Command and had the power of constables, could smooth the way and speed the journey as no other local person was able to do.

Sir Brian Tuke died in 1545. He left a postal system covering established routes in the face of financial difficulties and considerable obstacles placed by the farmers and innkeepers of the countryside. For his work he had been receiving 100 marks (£66 13s. 4d.) a year, and when the Privy Council took over his accounts it became evident that this fine example of a Tudor statesman had been spending heavily from his own resources to maintain the service. The claim put in by his executors for expenses amounted to £1,485, a very large sum by sixteenth century standards. History does not tell whether his children ever received it. Probably not, for the Tudor monarchs showed peculiar pettiness in settling debts of this kind. In any event, Sir Brian had become a wealthy man in the general service of the King, even if the office of Master of the Posts had been a liability. In the sharing out of monastic lands with which Henry VIII enriched himself and those who were loyal to him, Sir Brian Tuke had received considerable additions to his property from the estates of Waltham Abbey.

There is another feature of message-carrying at this time which merits description. The suppression of the monasteries by Henry VIII had provided estates for many families who were in Royal favour. They were often far from any of the few Post routes then running, and they found the carrier posts much too slow. These people sent their letters by their own servants.

The Northumberland Household Book, giving details of the way an aristocratic home was run in the early sixteenth century, shows that the principal families of the realm regarded message-taking over long distances as a quite normal part of the household routine.

One of the rules laid down says

> Whensoever any of his Lordship Servauntes be comaunded to ride on Message in Winter that every of theym be allowed for the tyme for his being furth in his jornay ijd for every meall and ob [½d.] for his baiting; and for his hors every day and night of his saide jornay iiijd, viz a penny for his baiting and iijd at night for his provounder. The whiche is in all for a man and his hors in the Dai in Winter viijd. if it be Etting-Day; and, if it be Fasting-Day, then ijd to be abated; the which is vjd. on a Fasting Day.

It will be seen that the fees payable to the Posts were very much greater than those obtainable by ordinary servants for the same sort of work, and the job, quite apart from its prestige as part of the Royal Household, must have proved very attractive to the men chosen for it.

2

THE TUDOR POSTS

O^N the death of Sir Brian Tuke, the title of the office was changed to Master of the Messengers, Runners, and Posts, and two men were appointed: John Mason and William Paget. No important details of their term of office have remained, except that Ordinances issued in 1555 show that the Posts of the Dover road were permanent. The Posts were permitted to have a monopoly of letting out horses to " Currors " (men riding on official business), and they were ordered to have a horn hanging at their door, or a sign bearing the emblem painted on it. The reason for this advertisement of the whereabouts of the Post house was that many people travelled by Post—the best way of insuring against losing the path or falling into the hands of footpads. The Posts had to maintain reserve horses for such distinguished travellers, who arrived as a sort of living mail. On official business, the fee for this guide service was ½d. per stage; for private persons, the rate was 4d. per stage for the guide and 2d. per stage for the horse. The 4d. fee was known as the Guide's Groat.

The difficulties of maintaining any sort of courier system in those days can be understood only if some idea of the conditions of the road are known. Briefly, they were appalling. The Romans left the country a heritage of magnificent roads, and they stood up to hard use for centuries, but by the Middle Ages they were overgrown and largely buried. The method of transport for goods was largely that of pack-horse, and horseback for travellers of wealth and position. Everyone else, if they travelled at all, went on foot.

For strategic purposes, however, a considerable amount of bridge-building was carried out. The monarch demanded that each manorial lord should carry out three duties: to bear arms when asked, to help in the building and maintenances of castles, and to care for the bridges on the King's highway. Many of the more patriotic families took a great pride in their bridges, and on the whole the multitude of rivers and streams of England offered no obstacle to the traveller.

The roads, on the other hand, were supposed to be the responsibility of the parishes through which they passed, and because it was everybody's business it became no one's responsibility. They were little more than wide tracks, a morass in winter and a honeycomb of hoof holes and ruts in summer. The general lack of any sense of responsibility about the roads is shown in an ancient court record of the late fifteenth century. It appears that an Aylesbury miller in 1499 dug a pit in the highway, 10 feet long, 8 feet broad, and 8 feet deep, in which a travelling glove-merchant was drowned one night. The local jury acquitted the miller of all blame, on the grounds that he had nowhere else to get the particular clay he needed. Doubtless the local citizens considered the miller's excuse an extremely pertinent one, and the glove-merchant just foolhardy to have been travelling on the roads at night.

The few light vehicles in existence were called " chares " or " cars ". They provided transport for womenfolk and the aged, for no man would have deigned to use any wheeled conveyance instead of a horse in those times. Even these carts could not be used to any great extent in winter or far from London, and a litter slung between two horses was the usual method of conveyance for those who could not ride a horse. The coach, a massive vehicle hauled by six horses, came into use in the middle of the sixteenth century, but it was impressive rather than useful. Although Queen Elizabeth made her Royal Progresses through her domain by coach, she often had to complete her journey by horseback while the coachmen struggled and heaved to bring the vehicle along later for the formal procession within the precincts of the towns.

During the reign of Philip and Mary, important Acts designed to improve the roads and make them safer for travellers were passed.

One such Act pointed out that, as

the highways were then very noisome and tedious to travel in,
and dangerous to all persons and carriages, every parish shall
annually elect two surveyors of the highways, to see that the
parishioners, according to their lands, abilities, farms &c., send
their carts, horses, men, and tools four days in every year for
mending the roads.

The theory was good, but no details of how much work was to
be done in that time was explained. Farmers sent their most decrepit
employees, who enjoyed a pleasant break from work if by any
chance they were sent on a fine day, or, as more usually happened,
crouched in the bushes while the rain poured down, the farmer
having decided that a period of weather when farm work was
impossible was as good as any time for the contribution to the
local road repairs. The only exception to this avoidance of the
spirit of the law was that the farmers would patch up the road
in the immediate vicinity of their fields for the benefit of their
own carts and animals.

Eight years after Elizabeth ascended the throne, John Mason
died. It seems that his partner, William Paget, had never been
particularly active, and Thomas Randolph was appointed to run
the posts as well as to continue his diplomatic work. Randolph is
variously described in documents of the period as " Post Master ",
" Master of the Queen's Posts and Couriers ", and " Master of
the Posts ", the vagueness suggesting that the position was not yet
sufficiently high to have the dignity of a precise and formal legal
description. The postal work was of secondary importance to
Randolph, for he had numerous diplomatic duties to carry out on
behalf of his Royal mistress, and his absences abroad were many
and frequent. He appointed a deputy, Robert Parmenter.

The office was, however, of profound political and personal
importance to the Sovereign, for, after Elizabeth's excommunica-
tion and the imprisonment of Mary Stuart, intrigue was rife and
attempts on the Queen's life were common. Walsingham,
Elizabeth's Secretary of State, watched the mails for evidence of
such plots, and such tricks as writing with alum or water were well
known to him. Suspicious letters were opened, their secrets

revealed or codes deciphered, and they were then sent on their way. Really ruthless methods to obtain information were often used. In 1562, for example, Sir William Cecil (afterwards Lord Burghley) engaged a couple of robbers to halt the messenger of the Spanish Ambassador near Gravesend. His letters were read in this, the only way of overcoming diplomatic immunity.

Despite the tacit understanding between Elizabeth and her Master of the Posts that the service should not be too universal or efficient, the routes of strategic importance carried mail at a remarkably fine pace when really necessary. By far the most efficient service was that on the Dover road, where Mason's ordinances had been strictly observed. The traditional route mentioned by Chaucer still ran from the Tabbard Inn, Southwark, but the Posts gained a little time by travelling by water as far as Dartford. They then took the road through Rochester, Sittingbourne, and Canterbury, at which towns horses were changed, and the seventy miles covered in about twelve hours.

One letter still extant, sent by Essex to Cecil in 1597, left Sandwich at 7 p.m. on 22 June. It was handed to the boatmen at Dartford at 4 a.m. on 23 June. With a favourable tide, it would have reached Cecil by 8 a.m. This letter was doubtless carried at the maximum possible pace, for it was marked, " Hast Hast post Hast with all speed and diligence for lyfe lyfe lyfe ". It also had a drawing of a gallows—an " urgent " sign which even an illiterate boy could understand.

Randolph was possibly incapable of improving the service of the Posts in view of the Queen's attitude, but he did do his utmost to provide the special Posts for State affairs, and also called a halt to the slackness which had long been jeopardising them. The Orders of the Lords of Her Majesty's Privy Council, issued from Westminster on 14 January 1583, were the first comprehensive regulations for a regular Post service based on a national scale. They not only indicate the very foundations on which the vast postal edifice of to-day has been built, but they give an insight into the various activities which it was at that time deemed necessary to regularise and control.

The principal regulations were as follows:

The man in charge of the Post Stage must live there in

person, and if he is found to be employing a deputy he will forthwith be removed.

Those riding Post shall not lawfully take the horses of any man but of the ordinary Posts whose commission ought to be signed by Her Majesty, three of her Council, the Lord Treasurer of England, the Earl Marshal of England, the Lord Governor of Berwick, or his deputy; the Lord President of the North, or his deputy; the Warden of the Northern Marshes, Her Majesty's secretary, or the Master of Posts.

The Post shall receive three halfpence a mile on the Queen's service, and twopence per mile when otherwise engaged.

Each Post must keep a bound book registering the names of all men riding Post, the number of horses, and the date of their orders.

If couriers are so numerous that the number of horses is insufficient, then the Post may hire extra mounts, and must be assisted by Mayors, constables and other officers to enable him to obtain them.

No man riding Post shall ride without a guide, who shall blow his horn whenever he meets company, passes through a town, or at least three times every mile.

All Posts shall be exempted from attendance at the Assizes, Inquests, Sessions and Musters.

In summer the Posts must run at seven miles an hour, and in the winter at five miles an hour.

The constant horn-blowing mentioned in this ordinance seems unnecessary until it is remembered that the whole district was expected to co-operate in helping the Post on its way, and no doubt the clarion call of the post-horn, especially at night, enabled the men at each stage to get a few minutes' advantage in harnessing another mount, preparing some refreshment and make ready for the journey within the fifteen minutes allowed. The warning note also enabled heavy carts or pack trains to pull to the side and give a clear passage.

The speed set down in the order is of a high standard, and on the face of it there is little evidence on the letters in the Public Record Office, with their series of times and dates scrawled on the front by the Posts at each stage, that it was often maintained. It must be remembered, however, that the edict referred to the rate of travel between Posts and did not suggest the overall average speed.

With the constant fear of invasion by Spain, the Post road to the West Country became of vital importance. Even after the Armada had been defeated the West Country ports remained in a state of alert for many years, and an intricate Post system connected the many small ports of Devon and Cornwall with the main Post artery from Plymouth to London. This ran via Staines, Bagshot, Hartley Wintney, Basingstoke, Andover, Shaftesbury, Sherborne, Crewkerne, Honiton, Exeter, and Ashburton. An extension went by ferry from Plymouth across the Tamar estuary to Looe, and then via St. Austell and Truro to Falmouth.

Randolph also organised a system of foot Posts as part of the Armada warning system. He ordered that in every parish of the shires on the coast someone living near the parish church should be appointed as a foot postman. This man received a fee of sixpence a week and had to be ready to run to the nearest Post town with news that the enemy galleons had been sighted. Here was yet another of the well-organised precautions designed to supplement the chain of beacons which straddled the hill-tops of the island during those exciting years of the Golden Age of England, and undoubtedly the foot Posts were of enormous value when the six weeks of skirmishes that took place in July and August of 1588, starting off at Plymouth and finishing as far away as the Firth of Forth, smashed the Armada to pieces. It enabled food, ammunition and reinforcements to be sent out from the ports of Hampshire and Sussex and kept Seymour's squadron cruising in the Straits of Dover informed of the progress of the enemy fleet. It also enabled the Government in London to have a full appreciation of the progress of the battle. The documents relating to the Armada give much evidence about the Posts of that time. A continual stream of letters went from the capital to the Navy in the West Country. Indeed, Howard and Drake doubtless regretted that a service existed which sent a steady supply of contradictory orders from their temperamental Royal mistress. One such letter, written by Walsingham on 9 June, countermanding previous orders, took a week to reach Plymouth, but Howard's protest, followed by the Queen's reply, came by 22 June, so that the first letter took over seven days, but the two-way subsequent correspondence took only eight days.

The sighting of the Armada off the Lizard came to Plymouth by land. It was of priceless advantage to Howard, waiting in Plymouth for news. Thereafter there must have been men riding post haste through southern England day and night as the battle developed. Drake kept up a continuous correspondence while at sea for week after week. A typical one, to Lord Seymour informing him about the battle, read as follows:

The 21st [July] we have them in chase. This letter, my honourable good Lord, is sent in haste. The fleet of the Spaniards is somewhat above 100 sails, many great ships, but truly I think not half men-of-war. Written aboard her Majesty's good ship the Revenge off of Start [Point], the 21st, late in the evening, 1588.

The address was: " To the Right Honourable the Lord Henry Seymour, Admiral of H.M.'s Navy in the Narrow Seas, or in absence to Sir Wm. Winter Kent, give these with speed. Haste, post haste."

And post haste that letter went, to ensure, along with scores of other messages about ammunition, food, and replacements to be organised along the south-east coast, that by cool-headed organisation the greatest menace in the country's history was smashed.

After the emergency was over the foot postman remained as a service for villages which had previously been virtually cut off from anything but haphazard information, and there is a striking parallel in the way that the network of telephone lines which were put down all over the British Isles during 1940 for the air raid and invasion-warning systems of the Royal Observer Corps and the army have since proved of great benefit to outlying villages tucked away on the lonelier areas of our coasts.

Incidentally, these Tudor foot Posts gave the name to the many inns which still have the name of " Running Footman ". They do not refer, as many people believe, to the athletic activities of some servant of a nearby manor, but to the devotion to duty of the foot Posts.

There is one feature of the Elizabethan Posts which bears pointing out, and that is the remarkable standard of literacy of the ordinary people. It is evident from the way in which involved instructions were written on the covers of the letters, and the instructions which meant that at each stage some form of clerical work such as entering the time of despatch had to be undertaken, that almost everyone was expected to be able to read and write. Nowhere are there any provisions in the regulations for permission for the rank and file of the postal services to approach a local functionary in order to obtain help in reading instructions. It is a sidelight on the rapidity with which England had emerged from the dark ages and the horrors of the Black Death which was probably unsurpassed in the known world of that time. Merchants and farmers, constables and innkeepers, soldiers and sailors were using the Posts, almost in spite of the declared restrictive policy of the Government as regards their public use, and the fact that they were available as a means of intercourse between the principal towns still further encouraged the flowering of education among the ordinary folk of the realm.

Sir Thomas Randolph died in 1590, and his successors, John Stanhope and his son, were given the warrant for the office of Postmaster for life. They continued the arrangements made by Randolph for the internal Posts, amplifying the regulations issued by the latter. One minor change necessitated by greater postal activity was to increase the minimum requirements of three horses at some of the busy stages. The trouble came from the fact that the numerous officials of the Court who were permitted to authorise transit of letters by Post were lavishly generous with their signatures on behalf of friends—an abuse of privilege which was to increase as the years went by, as a later chapter will show.

The carriage of private letters was dealt with in another Elizabethan proclamation of 1591, which ordered that no letters were to be sent to or from foreign countries except by the Posts. This must have been a blow to the two great private systems which were running at that time—the Merchant Strangers' Post and the

Merchant Adventurers' Post. The former was run by the foreign merchants in England, who flourished in East Anglia, Kent, and London. They were mostly Flemish, Italians, and French. Henry VIII, who had encouraged the activities of these foreign visitors, had also permitted them to run their own postal service to their colleagues abroad, and they did it so efficiently that many English merchants took advantage of the service.

The Merchant Strangers elected their own Postmaster, though after the death of the first one, Christian Suffling, in 1568, there was a quarrel about the successor. The Italians wanted an English Catholic to have the post; the Flemish merchants preferred a man named Raphael van den Putte. The Privy Council was asked to decide the question, and, not surprisingly, it decided against the Englishman whose religious beliefs made him politically suspect.

Comparatively little data about the Merchant Strangers' Post has been handed down to us, but the growing anxiety about privately run foreign mail systems in Tudor times which led up to the 1591 proclamation is evidence enough that it was handling a large amount of correspondence. For one thing, its sole purpose was to foster trade, and a business letter was treated as urgent. The King's Posts, on the other hand, accepted private letters on sufferance, and they were taken only if and when State papers were ready for carriage along the same route. Further, the Merchant Strangers' Post provided a service covering most of the known world. It was possible to send a letter to any of the great mercantile cities of Europe, and even to the merchants who had just then established themselves in the Indies and the New World.

The Merchant Adventurers' Post was run by Royal permission, which had been given to English merchants who had business houses overseas. This trading corporation had been founded in the thirteenth century for the purpose of commerce with the Netherlands. A corresponding corporation in England was called the Brotherhood of St. Thomas of Canterbury. The two groups eventually joined forces, and as the manufacture of English cloth grew it became a very wealthy organisation, the headquarters in London being augmented by branches in Newcastle, Exeter and Antwerp.

The Merchant Adventurers suspected that letters sent by the

couriers of their rivals, the Merchant Strangers, suffered unaccountable delays and were probably opened just as certainly as if they had been sent by the Royal Posts, and with greater damage to their business. They therefore organised their own service for the sake of secrecy and speed. It was by means of this postal service that the astonishing growth of English influence overseas was partly fostered. On the accession of Elizabeth, foreign trade was small; within a few years of the defeat of the Armada the tiny country had become a great trading nation as well as a powerful political entity. The couriers of the Merchant Adventurers, spreading their news farther and farther into the distant parts of the world, brought about this remarkable commercial expansion.

Shakespeare refers briefly to one of the greatest of these enterprises when one of the witches in *Macbeth* says: " Her husband's to Aleppo gone, master of the *Tiger* ". The *Tiger* took a party of merchant couriers to that town in 1583, armed with a charter from the Queen and the name of the Turkey Company. With them they took a letter from Elizabeth to Akbar, the Great Moghul. After imprisonment in Goa at the hands of the Portuguese, they eventually reached the Moghul's fabulous city of Fatehpur Sikri, and one of the party, Ralph Fitch, actually reached Burma.

Altogether Fitch was away eight years, and the letters he was able occasionally to send back, and the report he made when he once again returned to London, led to the founding of the East India Company, another example of a trading organisation which set up its own mail service as the life-blood of its great commercial system.

The strictly monopolistic character of the overseas trading organisation was probably one reason why Elizabeth wished to curtail foreign Posts not run under the control of the Crown or these monopolies. It was certainly not merely a formal order. Sheriffs were empowered to make " diligent search of all males, bougets [the leather pouch in which documents were carried by the Posts], and carriages of all private carriers ".

3

THE POSTS EXPAND

IT is surprising that the Posts made any advance at all during the early seventeenth century. James I was, of course, heartily disliked by both Parliament and the majority of the English population, but as he wisely left the running of the Posts largely in the hand of the Stanhopes, they continued much as they were in the last years of Elizabeth's reign. The Posts must have been very busy, for there now comes criticism of the profits which the Stanhopes were making out of their Patent through exorbitant fees demanded for appointments. To this charge they could reply that business was so good that Postmasters themselves farmed out their appointments, inferring that if everyone was doing well there was surely no harm in the men at the helm taking their share. Such an attitude to a public service may seem strange to modern ears, but at that time and for long afterwards these monopolies were regarded as quite normal perquisites of enterprise or, as more often applied, of friendships of the right kind in official quarters.

Although the Stanhopes had control of the mails both in Britain and overseas, the Merchant Adventurers still retained their privilege of running their own system, and when the Government tried to withdraw this right, business interests protested bitterly. This was not the only quarrel about the monopoly of the Posts at that time. James I granted a Patent to a Flemish merchant living in Britain, Mathew de Quester, to run the Posts to Europe outside the King's Dominions (these, so far as Europe was concerned, consisted solely of Calais). De Quester had been in charge of the Posts abroad in the position of employee, and this new order set him up on his own, much to the justifiable annoyance of the Stanhopes, who could do little, because the new Patent specifically stated that they were permitted to organise the mail services only in England and the Dominions. The elder Stanhope died while the quarrel went on, and finally it was decided that the de Quester concession to carry the foreign mails was lawful. For about six years Mathew de Quester, aided by his father, seems to have held at least a nominal monopoly, and only the die-hard section of the merchants trading with the Germanic coastal towns continued to ignore the regulations, a policy in which they were tacitly encouraged by Stanhope. Then, in 1632, de Quester died, and as his father was a very old man the Merchant Adventurers immediately put forward the names of two men acceptable to them. They were Thomas Witherings and William Frizell, the latter being the sleeping member of the partnership. His name gets its place in postal history chiefly on account of his accusations against Witherings in later years, for the two men quickly fell out, and Witherings held the monopoly of the foreign Posts by himself. This undoubtedly was just as the business men had hoped, for Witherings was himself a mercer, had considerable influence in Court, and was a wealthy man. He was no figurehead, but vigorously pursued a development policy which cut down the time of delivery between London and Antwerp from a fortnight to three days, and the couriers travelled day and night to give this extremely good service. It meant, of course, the use of the short sea route. The Posts rode day and night along the London-Dover road, a boatman was always standing by for the crossing to Calais, and from there along the coast there seems to have been an excellent Post organisation run for the benefit of Witherings by the French. No doubt he was able to use the foreign riders because he held a post in the entourage of the Queen of France.

The Dover road, incidentally, became impassable in bad weather except for pedestrians and horsemen, who could make wide detours to avoid the bogs and ruts. It is recorded that the household and retinue of Queen Henrietta, travelling along it in carts in 1640 on a visit to London, took four days on the journey from the coast to the capital, and this presumably with all the organisation which Witherings could put into operation on behalf of the Queen.

The efficiency and regularity of the Posts run by Witherings over such roads must have made a thought-provoking comparison with the internal services. In theory, the mail routes then in existence were quite widespread and capable of delivering letters at a fine turn of speed when urgency spurred the riders on, but in practice they were erratic and unreliable. The basis on which they were organised had been completed some years before, while Elizabeth was still on the throne.

In 1598 the temporary Posts were discontinued and fixed routes set up to Ireland via Holyhead, and another route via Bristol and Milford Haven.

The stages on the London-Holyhead route were at Barnet, St. Albans, Brickhill, Towcester, Daventry, Coventry, Coleshill, Lichfield, Stone, Nantwich, Chester, Rhuddlan, Conway and Beaumaris. The distance of 275 miles was covered in 1598 at an average of nearly five miles an hour, which is very good for a journey with considerable night travel and hilly country in the final stages of the route.

Two vessels were kept at Holyhead and Dublin to maintain a shuttle service, and given a fair wind a letter could go from London to Ireland in seventy-two hours.

The second route gave a much shorter land journey, but a longer sea route, and avoided the troubles of Irish roads, if the message was intended for southern Ireland. The stages from London were Hounslow, Maidenhead, Reading, Newbury, Marlborough, Chippenham, Marshfield, Bristol, Newport, Cardiff, Bridgend, Swansea, Carmarthen, Haverfordwest, and Dale. This route was abandoned some twenty years later.

In 1603 a fixed Post to Berwick-on-Tweed and Scotland was organised. This was a great achievement if the stages were maintained summer and winter, as they seem to have been. There are records showing that a letter took sixteen hours to cover the road between Durham and Newcastle — a distance of some fifteen miles—which is indicative of bad winter conditions.

The route for the London-Berwick post is virtually the Great North Road of to-day. The stages were London, Waltham Abbey, Ware, Royston, Caxton, Huntingdon, Stilton, Stamford, South Witham, Grantham, Newark, Tuxford, Scrooby, Doncaster, Ferrybridge, Wetherby, Boroughbridge, Northallerton, Darlington,

Durham, Newcastle, Morpeth, Alnwick, Belford, and Berwick. A branch also went westwards from Newcastle through Hexham to Carlisle. In the northern sections the road was bad and the stages slow, but on occasion remarkable speeds were evidently possible.

For an instance of such speedy travel along the Post roads we cannot find a better example than that of Sir Robert Carey, who was given the order to convey the news of the death of Queen Elizabeth to James VI of Scotland in Edinburgh. Carey left London on the morning of 25 March 1603, and was in Doncaster, 160 miles distant, the same night. Two more days were taken to reach Edinburgh, and he galloped through the streets of the Scottish capital late that night, when James was already in bed. The ride, undertaken at a time when there are twelve hours of darkness in the twenty-four, had covered 410 miles in under sixty hours, an average speed by one man of nearly seven miles an hour. It was an achievement that puts the far less authentic and shorter gallop of Dick Turpin in the shade, and it was possible because of the smooth-running organisation of the Post at every stage on that memorable journey, which had fresh mounts and guides ready for duty.

Under James I, John Stanhope and his son Charles were regranted the position of Masters of the Post, while Postmasters on the route south which had been taken by the Royal cavalcade from Scotland received recognition of their services. James stopped the night at the post-house at Scrooby, and the hospitality he received resulted in the Postmaster there, William Brewster, being granted an increase of wages to 2s. a day.

There were also many unofficial Posts in operation, details of which have been lost in most instances. For example, in 1620 a Post to Plymouth was set up to oust a private system which was run on the same route by a man named Jude. For some time, according to Post Office records, the official and unofficial posts ran side by side, and in 1629, under the stimulant of this healthy competition, the King's Post undertook to carry letters once a week along the Plymouth route—and to deliver them within twenty miles of the road without extra charge.

Such was the general picture before 31 July 1635, when

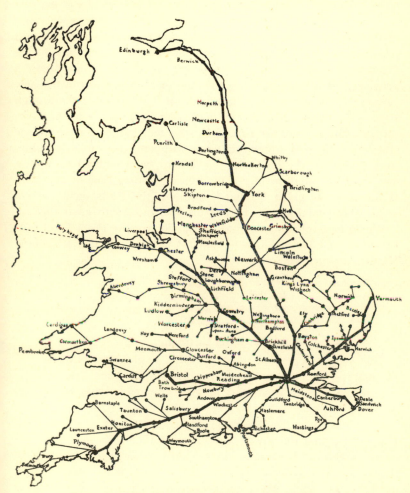

MAIL ROUTES AND POST TOWNS ORGANISED BY
THOMAS WITHERINGS, 1635-51.

Charles I issued a proclamation organising the Posts of England and Scotland, probably based on a plan formulated by Secretary Coke. It was a notable landmark in postal history, for it marked the recognition by the Crown of the essentially public service side of the Posts. From being an official courier system which would take commercial and private communications if convenient, the Posts were now to be run for people as a right rather than a privilege. It is not surprising that the man chosen to run the new system was the official who had made such a success of the foreign Posts—Thomas Witherings. He had reached eminence in the Posts through intrigue on his behalf by the merchants against the de Questers. He now found his work hampered by similar troubles from Stanhope, the holder of the Patent, who realised he was in danger of becoming merely a figurehead. For a time at any rate, Witherings was given his head, and ran the Posts on a version of his Continental system and at his own rates with great success.

Witherings' scheme was that he should pay the Posts 3d. a mile (a total of £2,350 in all) and that for this they carried all letters. His own charges would be:

> 2d. per letter up to 80 miles.
> 4d. per letter up to 140 miles.
> 6d. per letter above 140 miles.
> 8d. per letter to Scotland.
> 9d. per letter to Ireland.

The service operated on six Post roads from London—to Edinburgh, Holyhead, Plymouth, Bristol, Norwich, and Dover. Branch Posts were organised to meet the main Posts in various provincial towns.

The Crown had the advantage of being relieved of all responsibility of running the Posts, as well as of their cost, which on the previous system of irregular despatches and inconsiderate abuse of the services available had proved very heavy. It was evident very quickly that, while everyone benefited—the Crown by economy and the public by the provision of a regular service—Witherings did best of all. He made a fortune out of his scheme. It was a striking contrast to the financial position of the Posts in 1609, when they were run at a loss of £3,400.

Witherings lasted in office for two years. His dismissal was

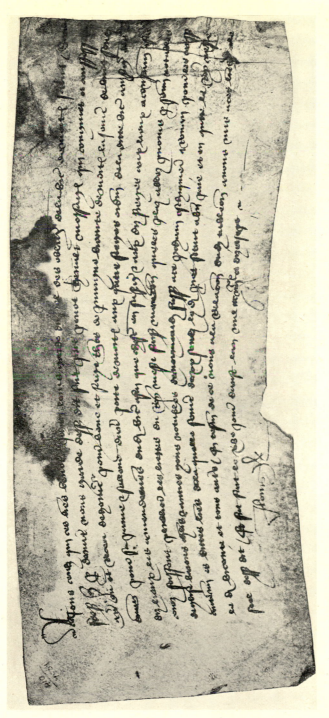

Before 1482 no postal organisation existed in England. Those wishing to send letters had to find their own messengers and pay their expenses. The above is a receipt from such a messenger, acknowledging payment for carrying letters for the Vicomte de Mortain in 1397.

BRIANVS TVKE. MILES,   AN ETATIS SVÆ. LVII

DROIT ET   AVANT.

SIR BRIAN TUKE

A Tudor Posts pay warrant. It is an account of the expenses incurred by a messenger of Queen Elizabeth for taking letters into Norfolk in 1565.

An order issued by Sir Brian Tuke in 1537, in his position as Treasurer of the King's Chamber, for the engagement of mounted Posts between Waltham Cross and Lincoln. For an explanation see footnote on inextricably mixed up in the political troubles which had then started between Charles I and Parliament, but no direct charges of inefficiency could be found to lay against the man who, more than any other, created a worthwhile postal service for the United Kingdom many decades ahead of any other country. The futility of the complaints against him is shown from the fact that he actually lost the job because he was not an aristocrat and could not speak foreign languages. Needless to state, his erstwhile partner, Frizell, emerged from obscurity to voice these charges.

An amelioration of this seeming injustice of the Secretaries of State who organised the dismissal is that Witherings was a King's man, by virtue of the office he held, if not in his personal views as well. Parliament was rightly becoming wary of encouraging offices which were monopolies bestowed by Royal favour and capable of gross mismanagement and corruption without the representatives of the people being able to do much about it. Moreover, the post-masters and the rank and file were restless and dissatisfied. The honest officials were literally in danger of being ruined by the mere fact of holding office. They were compelled to maintain horses and postboys by law, but their wages were months and even years in arrears; some of them being in prison for debt. The more ruthless and dishonest members started mail-carrying and post-horse hiring as a private business on their own acount, charging whatever the market would bear. This type of postmaster doubtless

---

(Transcription of facing plate)

9th October, 1536.

All ye the marres constables balyffes and other good officers of the towns of Waltham Crosse Ware Royston Huntyngdon Stylton Stamford Slyford and Lyncoln ye shall understand the kynges pleasour is that incontynently upon the seight herof ye shall appoynt an able man well horsed in the sayd towns to lye in post and to carye by night or day all such letters as shall be sent by there handes to or from the kynges highness or his most venerable counsale from post to post that is to say eny post to the next post for the wyche ye shall have at my handes for eny of thym xiid by day as long as they shall lye so in post and the post of Waltham must goo furthe incontynently to Ware with thys byll to lay the post there and the post of Ware lykwysse to Royston and so eny post must carye thys byll to the kynges officers to the next of the next of the sayd towns outward so to lay the post wythout tarying in any place but to do it in all dyligence and the post of Waltham to bryng his lres suthward to the post of London fale ye not herof at your uttermost perill at London the vith day of Octobre the xxviiith yere of our Sovereign Lord kyng Henry the VIIIth

Brian Tuke Kynght, Treasorer of the kyngs chambour.

felt quite happy that the disorganisation should continue. His
more honest colleague noted that Witherings was advocating all
kinds of changes, the net results of which for a man of probity
would be more calls on his time and resources without any sign
of prompt and regular payment of wages.

It could not be expected that a man running a lonely Post deep
in the West Country could appreciate that such payments were not
the concern of Witherings, but still under the charge of Stanhope.
The arrears of wages exceeded £60,000 when the Witherings
scheme started, and, apart from payments to the more vociferous
complainants, nothing seems to have been put right before the
country was plunged into civil war.

In the darkening months before the clash came the Posts became
more deeply involved in the moves and counter-moves of Parliament and the Crown. By 1640 Charles I had appointed a
naturalised subject named Burlamachi to the position held by
Witherings. This instantly aroused the wrath of Parliament. They
might well have gained a victory if both Houses could have agreed
about their nominee, but in fact the Commons and the Lords were
as bitterly opposed to each other as both were to the King over
the person who should hold the office. The Lords backed
Witherings, because he had by then assigned his office to the Earl
of Warwick, and the Commons put forward one of their own
members, Edmond Prideaux, a native of Norfolk. In this three-
cornered fight, Burlamachi was the first one to be vanquished.
Warwick and Prideaux seem to have then competed for the office
on their theory that possession is nine points of the law, and groups
of men ranged out from London to grab the mail on the final Post
stages. Sometimes the bags changed hands twice in the last twenty
miles of its journey, but it was always delivered, presumably
because neither side wished to have any charge of tampering with
the letters laid against it.

Inevitably, after civil war broke out, Prideaux became the man
that mattered. It was he who organised a military courier system
to keep Cromwell in touch with the situation throughout the
country, and it is to his credit that even in such turbulent times
he seems to have managed to get the normal Posts running before
the war ended. His services to the Roundheads were recognised

by his appointment as Attorney-General after the execution of Charles I, and the position of Postmaster-General was then put up for auction—the farming system by which regulations had to be obeyed but profits could be retained by the holder. How valuable the office was can be gathered from the fact that the winning bid, from John Manley, was about £10,000.

4

THE POSTS UNDER THE MONOPOLY

WHEN John Manley took over the Posts in the summer of 1653, he had to put down a number of minor postal services which were running at lower rates than the official one. Some of these schemes had been started by men who felt deeply that the monopolistic character of the Post Office was bad and that the farming of the system was an unreasonable privilege. Others had been maintained by these postmasters who had found years before that a good living was to be made by running a local service. They could make a profit even though they charged lower rates than the official ones. Prideaux had done his utmost to stop these rival Posts, even resorting to physical violence on the postmen concerned, and he had also capitalised on the Puritanical trends of his day by demanding that the justices of the peace should prevent postmen working on the Sabbath—that is, all competing postmen, for those of Prideaux did not ride on Sundays, while this was one of the attractions of the " Pirate Posts ".

There was even the germ of an idea of a penny post at this time put forward by a Yorkshireman named John Hill (no relation of the pioneer of the actual penny post in 1840, Rowland Hill). His idea was to carry letters in England for 1*d*. and to Scotland for 2*d*. This scheme was merely outlined in a pamphlet and was not put into operation, but at the time of Manley's appointment Hill was certainly running his own postal service over a wide area around York at very low rates.

Once again the majesty of the law was invoked to protect the postal monopoly. In 1654 Cromwell, now Lord Protector of the

Commonwealth, signed an ordinance which forbade any unauthorised person to set up a postal service, keep horses for the Posts, or run a mail boat. It also ordered the Tudor speed of seven miles an hour in summer and five in winter to be maintained, and there was a warning that changes at the Post stages should not take more than fifteen minutes. The rest of it was a repetition of the Elizabethan proclamation.

Other instructions issued later by Cromwell indicate that he was tempted to use the Posts as an espionage service. Disaffection was naturally rife, and, apart from any tampering with the letters from people in the Royalists' areas or from persons who had been on the Royalists' side (assuming that they were foolish enough to trust their writings to the Posts), situation reports on the area had to be sent to London. Although there are no precise details of the changes of the postmasters along the roads, we can assume that those who had been appointed through Royal influence had long before been dismissed, and no doubt the majority of those then working could be trusted with confidential instructions about espionage because their appointments were rewards for services rendered during the war.

John Manley retained his appointment for two years, when John Thurloe, Secretary of State, paid £10,000 for the rights. Cromwell's statement confirming this appointment mentioned that one reason for it was the security of the country, which was generally speaking returning to normal conditions, and the Posts accordingly flourished. By the time of the Restoration the annual rent required was £21,500, and even at this figure the competition to obtain the farm indicates that it was a most profitable investment for the holder. The winner was a man from Henfield, Sussex, Henry Bishop, who had been interested in the Posts under Cromwell.

Although the first great Post Office legislation was that of Cromwell in 1657, the end of the Protector's regime soon afterwards resulted in the fact that it is Charles II who makes a great contribution to this particular section of our history. It was fundamental principle of his reign that the laws passed under the Protectorate were void, so that all the Post Office ordinances of that era—they had not in any case been very revolutionary—were after 1660 unenforceable in law. Charles II asked Parliament to pass a Post Office Act which was both comprehensive and sensible. The principal executive change was that the Postmaster-General was appointed for a term of years (he still paid a rent for the privilege), and this enabled a man with probity and ideas really to develop the schemes he had in mind. Previously, the risk, and even likelihood, that the job would disappear at the end of twelve months curtailed initiative.

One interesting point about the clauses which concerned foreign mails is the long distances over which it was now possible to send a letter. The principal towns of France, Northern Germany, and Italy were listed, indicating that Posts were by now a normal feature of life in Europe as well as England, though the method of international payment for the Posts' service is not clear. Often the problem was, of course, solved by charging the recipient, but as the Charter specifically mentions inward rates from Paris and Antwerp, some sort of agreement with the foreign postal services must have been reached.

When this Act was passed, many changes were again made among the provincial postmasters. Those who had been expelled from their offices by Cromwell successfully applied for reinstatement. A notable exception to the insecurity which the existing office-holders held was that of Henry Bishop himself, the Postmaster-General. Although he had been appointed before the Restoration, he was allowed to remain in office—for three years. Then there were charges that he had retained enemies of the King in the Post Office service, and he resigned.

Bishop introduced a postmark stamp for letters as a check on his employees. He also opened five letter-reception offices between Westminster and Ludgate and seems to have applied himself vigorously to the task of improving the service.

We have noted how at intervals from the reign of Henry VIII public-spirited men did their utmost to organise the Posts as a great public service. True, most of them achieved wealth and some even fame by so doing. These tangible rewards were deserved for the efforts which they made to overcome the attitude that the Posts were primarily a useful source of revenue, to be maintained just sufficiently well to keep the moneys coming in and to prevent the automatic growth of private services.

Unfortunately, the cycle of history was now to repeat itself, and the statesmanlike but spendthrift Charles II began to mulct the Post Office of money which, at any other time than this vigorous expansion of natural and economic life, might have jeopardised the very existence of the system. There is little doubt that Bishop found the expected profits smaller than the figures had led him to believe, due to the liberal use of franks (free letters for Members of Parliament and other officials), and for that reason he did not make any great effort to retain his office. His successor, Daniel O'Neile, who paid his £21,000 to the King and took over from Bishop in 1663, is worthy of mention because it was during his tenure of office that London suffered the two years of horror of the Plague, culminating in the Great Fire. In 1665 two-thirds of the staff of forty-five in the Inland and Foreign Letter Offices in London either deserted their posts or died. It is, of course, improbable that a parasite-born disease brought many risks of contagion to the staff from handling the mails, and the incidence of death among the Post Office personnel must be only too typical of the general figures in any office in London at that time. Actually the letters were fumigated with steam and various noisome mixtures boiled in the cauldrons over which they were held, and it is remarkable that their superscriptions and contents were readable afterwards. However that may be, the mail service continued, brave men continued to ride to and from the capital with the Posts, and no move was made to evacuate the mainspring of the postal organisation to a safer area outside the stricken city.

Postal affairs were at that time conducted from two houses. The Foreign Letter Office was in Love Lane, not far from London Bridge, and the inland mails were handled in Cloak Lane, Dowgate. Both were within a few hundred yards of the site of the outbreak of the Great Fire in Pudding Lane. Within two days both had been utterly destroyed. After the Fire a temporary office was opened in the Black Pillars Tavern, Covent Garden, a move far beyond the borders of the city, which indicates how complete must have been the desolation there. The accommodation was purely temporary, and as soon as a building was available the offices moved to Bishopgate.

Shortly after O'Neile was appointed Postmaster-General, Charles II managed to persuade Parliament to pass an Act settling the profits of the Post Office on his brother, the Duke of York, and his heirs. Revenues under the farming system consisted of the annual rents paid by the farmers and the sums paid by the officials for their appointments which had to be renewed from time to time. Farmers in theory retained the postage revenues they could extract from the postmasters. It was a heavy burden for the Posts to have to pay the Duke of York as well as the farmer, but the immense growth in the volume of letters passing over its road system seems to have been able to stand this admirably. The annual rent rose steadily in value, reaching £43,000 a year by 1680, while the profits taken by the Duke of York were about £65,000 when he ascended the throne as James II in 1685. Incidentally, these hereditary revenues continued to be paid to the Crown until the accession of George III.

Nor were these the only financial penalties imposed before the postal revenue could be used for improvements and expansion. The Post became a purse into which the royal hand could regularly and generously dip for costly presents and pensions. The Duchess of Cleveland, mistress of Charles II, received £4,700 from the Post Office profits and continued to do so until her death in 1709, when her son, the Duke of Grafton, the illegitimate child of Charles, received it, and this annual payment continued to his heirs until less than a century ago, when it was commuted for £91,000. Many other members of the nobility, as well as minor personalities of the Court and Post Office, received pensions ranging from £200 to £2,000 a year, and by the end of the century something like a quarter of the total revenue from the Posts was being spent in this way.

Much of this chapter has been concerned with the internal affairs of the Post Office. It is the principal feature of this period of its history, for the growing volume of the Posts had made the position of the Postmaster-General an important one politically, as well as a source of wealth. The actual machine was largely left to run itself, and the law of supply and demand at least ensured a rough-and-ready efficiency for which the rank and file of the Posts can take much credit. They are all the more to be commended because on occasion they were the principal sufferers in the fervid campaign to keep up with the pensions, grants, and so forth and to guarantee the Postmasters-General some return on the heavy rents they paid. Lord Arlington, for instance, who, as an intimate friend of Charles II (his daughter married the Duke of Grafton), had been appointed in succession to O'Neile in 1667 and retained the position for life (paying a rent rising from £25,000 to £43,000 for the concession), ruthlessly slashed wages and imposed enforced payments which to-day would be regarded as bribes. The weekly wages of letter-carriers in London were cut to 6s. and the post-masters in the provincial towns had to pay a year's salary (£40 in most cases) in order to retain their jobs. Once again the reaction must be one of amazement that the Posts continued to expand in such circumstances, but expand they did, and more and more letters poured into the receiving offices. One protection that the public had was that postage rates could not be raised, and this was not altered until the important Act was passed in 1711, in the reign of Queen Anne, at a time when the Post Office revenue had grown to £111,461.

In 1695 an Act of the Scottish Parliament had set up a separate Post Office and Postmaster-General for Scotland, but in 1711, by the English Act, dealing with all matters connected with the Post Office, the two offices and officers were re-united. The rates of postages were varied by this Act, as they were often varied subsequently, but they were still calculated on the principle of distance, originated by Witherings, and the minimum rate 3d. applied up to 80 miles. A certain proportion of the revenue of the Post was now to go to the public Exchequer; the remainder to the Crown. The increase in the postage rates was for the purpose of providing funds for the war with France and Spain then in progress, and it was provided that for a term of thirty-two years " the weekly sum of £700 out of the duties and revenues arising by virtue of this Act shall be paid by the Postmaster-General into the Exchequer upon Tuesday in every week ". Further, one-third of any surplus over and above the revenue at the old rates, after

2

the payment of £700 weekly, was reserved to the disposal of Parliament.

The anticipated increase of revenue was, however, hardly realised. A return of Post Office income and expenditure called for by the Treasury in 1721 showed that, compared with 1710, the increase in the net revenue was about £33,000 a year, as against the minimum of £700 a week (£36,400 a year) expected by the framers of the Act. The weekly sum of £700 had, however, been regularly paid into the Exchequer, and the loss therefore fell on the Crown.

The Act of 1711, if unsuccessful in one direction, had important financial results in another. One of its clauses provided for the creation of cross-Posts, up to that time practically non-existent. By the year 1719 the postage on by-Post and cross-Post letters amounted to £4,000, and in that year Ralph Allen, Postmaster of Bath, offered to take the by-Posts and cross-Posts on lease at a rent of £6,000 a year. The contract granted on these terms, and renewed from time to time, was estimated by Allen to have brought him an aggregate profit of £500,000. The source of this sum—the letters which never passed through London—brings us to the next important phase of Post Office history.

5
LOCAL AND PROVINCIAL POSTS

PROVINCIAL folk, with some justification often complain even to-day that in matters of legislation and the organisation of public service London is regarded as almost the be-all and end-all of the nation's life. This was certainly true of the Posts up to the time that Charles II came to the throne. The Post covered many hundreds of miles and passed through scores of towns and villages, but the routes went mostly from London and the towns with Posts were serviced merely because they lay along these roads and not because of their importance. Branches from the main roads were not very numerous. Towns which did not happen to be in the right place simply went without any Royal Mail, though the very fact of their size and activity created an official and technically illegal service. The carriers, as we have noted, conveyed letters long distances, and by the comradeship of these men of the road a letter could be handed from inn to inn to reach almost any part of the country in due time.

For more localised journeys the usual postman was the pedlar or higgler. There were many thousands of these packmen on the roads of Britain at this time, carrying their wares from door to door and working up a profitable clientele. Some of them followed an eight months' route which took them to the great fairs, which started as early as March in King's Lynn and continued without cessation in every town and large village of the country until the Nottingham Goose Fair of late autumn. Others—these were the unofficial postmen—made up a regular circuit, which they simply plodded round in order to call on their customers every two months or so. These men would regard twenty-five miles a day with as much as forty pounds of cloth, hardware, and similar household goods in their packs as quite ordinary, and they also carried large quantities of letters from customer to customer. As it was a sideline, the main purpose of which was to create goodwill, their charges were low. Even on the main Post routes these pedlars carried mail, and sometimes they would deliver it more quickly than the official service. The reason for this was that, even when two towns were on existing Post routes, their letters would have to go to London for sorting—and pay for the actual journey of several hundred miles even though the geographical distance between the two places was only fifty miles or so.

The crying need for cross-country Posts was met in 1660 with the institution of the by-Post system—the carriage of mails along the by-ways. Sheffield, Derby, and Lincoln were typical of the towns which had previously been isolated and were now provided with connections to the nearest point on the trunk postal routes. By the end of the seventeenth century smaller towns like Stratford-on-Avon, Shrewsbury, and Coventry were included in the growing network of by-Posts. A parallel development was the local Post for larger towns. The best was that in London, created in the face of considerable opposition from official sources by William Dockwra, a merchant. It was a Penny Post, and for this sum he offered to carry letters and small packets to and from any parish in the cities of London and Westminster, the maximum distance so covered being about seven miles. In his introductory announcement, Dockwra with truth described it as " A Penny Well Bestowed ". He must have had considerable organising ability, for on an April day in 1680 Londoners found that hundreds of taverns and shops had hung out notices announcing that letters for the Penny Post were taken there. Delivery time was better than anything that can be offered even to-day, for Dockwra's messengers collected the mail from these receiving stations as often as once every hour of daylight on weekdays, at the same time delivering mail addressed to these stations. There were sorting offices near Newgate Street, in Smithfield, Southwark, and St. Martin's Lane. The letters were stamped in the sorting office with a postmark giving the initial of the office, time, and date.

As shown by the developments that came 160 years later, the

most astonishing feature of the Dockwra Post was the use of a flat rate of postage, irrespective of distance, and (up to a pound) of weight. It would seem that this pioneer had hit on the best system of simplification of the actual accounting and clerical side of postal work long before Rowland Hill fought so hard for the same idea.

It will be realised that Dockwra was sailing dangerously close to the wind as regards contravening the rules of the Crown's monopoly of the Posts. He aggravated the situation by improving the service by collecting incoming letters from the General Post Office and also delivering outgoing mail there for forwarding to the provinces. No doubt the volume of business he was doing in this way was duly reported by the clerks to their superiors, and after the Dockwra Penny Post had been running for two years the Duke of York, by then owner of the Post Office concession, started a series of lawsuits to restrain him. It must have taken some courage to stand up to a brother of the King, but Dockwra did so, even though the damages being asked for totalled £10,000. The doughty defendant protested in court that his system had increased the business of the Royal Mail (which was true because of his service of carrying local letters for forwarding over the official routes), and he also brought forward a rather nebulous defence that, as it was a proposition for the common weal, working by a method entirely different from the General Post, it deserved and was legally authorised to continue. Not surprisingly, the judge decided it wasn't, and nominal damages were awarded against him. It might be expected that there would have been an outcry from the people of London which would have made such a decision politically unwise, but it must be remembered that there was no Parliament in 1682, as Charles II was ruling in a state of virtual autocracy. More than that, many hundreds of the poor who had managed to make a bare living by working as messengers for the commercial houses had lost their jobs through the Dockwra system, and these men had not been slow to attack the Dockwra postmen with violence. With them, at least, the decision on the King's Bench was good news—or so they thought. Within a month, however, of Dockwra being compelled to cease his activities the London Penny Post was in operation once more—this time under the Royal Arms. It rapidly grew with an almost identical routine with which it had started. Within a few years there were more than fifty messengers making their hourly rounds of the despatch and reception offices. Their pay was 1s. 4d. a day, and it is easy to see that profits for the Post Office must have been considerable.

Dockwra, who had a wife and eight children, appealed to Parliament under James II for redress by the restoration of the concession to him or the granting of a pension. He was voted £500 for seven years, and this tardy recognition of his contribution to the progress of the Royal Mail was further enhanced in 1696, when he was appointed Controller of the Penny Post at a salary of £200 a year on top of his pension. It looked as if things were at last put right, but intrigue against him continued. There were charges that he reduced the revenue (as a matter of interest, the revenue increased from £3,623 to £3,884 during his tenure of office), that he was ill-tempered, and that he would not allow the messengers to accept large parcels. The pettiness of the charges was not evident to his critics. He was dismissed and his pension stopped. Sickened by the state of affairs, Dockwra later emigrated to New Jersey, where an efficient postal service was inaugurated about the same time. There is no evidence that Dockwra was directly connected with this, but it would seem that he must certainly have been the guiding force during the remainder of his life. He died in 1716, still unhonoured, as many pioneers have been.

By 1663, many towns off the main routes were getting their mail. It was then stated: " with each mail or packet there goes a bybag which is carried by the Post boy about his middle in which all letters are put, that is, such letters as are sent from one town to another upon the roads, which never come near the Office ". This must have meant that letters from towns en route were made up separately. There is no justification for believing that they concerned towns lying off the Post route. According to the official history of the Post Office of that period, there were only two cross-Posts in 1710, as distinct from branch routes of the main London roads. They connected Exeter and Chester and Bath and Oxford.

One youngster in the West Country was thinking a lot about local letters at this time. He was Ralph Allen, who assisted his grandmother, the Postmistress at St. Columb, a Post set up to connect with the Plymouth stage. At the time of the 1710 developments he was a youth of sixteen. Allen became one of the most notable of the citizens of Bath in those years when the town was the Mecca of fashion and the arts. For a vivid portrait of the man, it is worth while studying the character of Squire Allworthy in Fielding's *Tom Jones*, for this is really Allen, wealthy stone-quarry-owner, friend of Royalty, Mayor of Bath, and Postmaster of the city when it was one of the most important provincial mail centres in the country.

Allen saw the possibilities for developing the cross-Posts as a valuable public service, and also, it must be conceded, as a means of making a fortune for himself. He obtained the right to run the country's cross-Posts for seven years. This was in 1720, and the contract was periodically renewed for the rest of his long life. He offered £2,000 a year more than the actual revenue when he took over, indicative of his faith in the way it could be developed. As it happened, he lost money on the first contract, but in this preparatory period he steadily went on organising routes. By the middle of the century there were cross-Posts serving such widely scattered and hitherto lonely isolated places as Ely, Wells-next-the-Sea, King's Lynn, and Bury St. Edmunds in East Anglia; Halifax, Skipton, Hull, Scarborough, and Whitby in the North; Kidderminster, Wolverhampton, Leicester, and Derby in the Midlands; East Grinstead, Alton, Guildford, and Shaftesbury in the South; Bridgwater, Barnstaple, and Launceston in the West. Only in the north-west of England, Wales and Scotland was there any town of any importance without a service on three days a week, and the majority had a six-days-a-week schedule.

The first town to start a Penny Post after authority was given in 1764 was Dublin. It began operating in 1773, but for many years hardly justified its existence by the volume of letters carried, and it would appear that enthusiasm to make a really comprehensive organisation had created much too involved a network. There were more than eighty reception and despatch stations, some only taking in four or five letters a week, despite four calls a day from the messengers.

In Edinburgh, the second town to adopt the Penny Post, it was

CROSS-POSTS ESTABLISHED BY RALPH ALLEN 1721-61.

much more successful. A man named Williamson, who owned a coffee-house, had been providing his customers with a sort of *poste restante* service as early as 1770. He received so many requests to "let Mr. —— have this letter when he comes in" that by 1776 he had started a proper messenger service and publicised it so that it could be used by others as well as his customers. His couriers wore a uniform and, like the criers, went through the streets with bells so that people could run out and put the mail in their hands as well as delivering them to various offices. As the Scottish postal service had definitely been under the direct control of London since 1710, it is remarkable that no objections were made to Williamson's service on the monopoly question, and when the official Penny Post was started in Edinburgh in 1793 the Scottish pioneer was given a small pension by way of compensation, and his "rights" of providing a limited service respected.

Because of the growing industrial importance of other towns as the Industrial Revolution increased their size rapidly and made the amount of business correspondence of justifiable size to warrant a service, the Penny Post spread. Bristol, Manchester, Glasgow and Aberdeen were running them successfully in the early years of the nineteenth century.

The threads of the spider's web of postal routes over the map of England were filled in during the eighteenth century. There were numerous radial lines centred on London, stretching through every important town in the country, and across the Border to Edinburgh. Gradually the links between these were joined by the route from one provincial town to another until, on a small-scale map, the system seemed remarkably comprehensive. But in terms of population there were still large numbers of rural people with no postal service at all. Before the coming of the railway with its cheap travelling facilities, a village twenty miles distant from a Post town was to all intents and purposes cut off from regular communication if it did not happen to be near the main road along which the mail coaches ran. The only regular journey undertaken by the inhabitants was to the nearest market town, and these were by no means all situated on the trunk routes. Children who went to work 100 miles away were almost as separated as if they had gone abroad.

Up to 1764 the Post Office carried letters to Post towns only, and it did not undertake, outside London, to deliver mail to the houses of the recipients. In 1764 the Postmaster-General obtained authority to set up in any town a Penny Post of the same type as the London system, and ten years later a decision of the Court of King's Bench ruled that within the limits of a Post town (limits which the Post Office should decide) letters should be delivered to the house of the recipient free of charge. The limit was usually ten miles, extended in 1794, but only in half a dozen towns was this facility provided in practice.

The rural inhabitants of the country still did not benefit by an extension of the postal services. They mostly had to set up their own organisation to collect and deliver the mail at the nearest Post town. Very often a pauper was employed for the job. He was paid a small wage, which was supplemented by a penny for each letter he carried. This was the arrangement for ordinary folk. Wealthy people could send one of their own footmen or they could arrange with the postmaster to collect and deliver for a small fee. As a matter of fact, many postmasters built up this private delivery arrangement into quite a lucrative sideline for themselves as time went on. John Byrom, the Manchester diarist, shorthand pioneer, and poet, whose letters to his wife and friends in his native town while he resided in London and others towns are in themselves a testimony to the reliability of the posts of the early eighteenth century, recounts an interesting story about the Manchester Postmaster. That gentleman had allegedly been mishandling letters and certainly making a private business of delivering some of them.

The incident, which is recounted in *Selections from the Journals and Papers of John Byrom*, edited by Henri Talon (Rockliff, 1950), is related to Byrom's wife in a letter dated 16 June 1737:

My dear L.[ove]: Mr. Charles Stanhope [Secretary to the Treasury] sent for me this morning to ask me if I knew the postmaster of Manchester, and whether I had heard any complaints against him for not delivering letters: making people wait that would not pay an halfpenny a letter that he had demanded, &c.; he said there was an affidavit lodged against him, and some other particulars he mentioned of a private nature. I told him that I did know the man, that I looked upon him to be a very honest man, that I had never heard of any complaints, unless it was something about taking a halfpenny, which I believed was not at present insisted on . . .

The reply which came from Byrom's wife indicated that the whole thing was rather a storm in a teacup, but there was an incidental comment which provides a useful insight into the more or less unofficial facilities which existed in provincial towns. Mrs. Byrom saw the Manchester Postmaster and told him of the complaints of Whitehall. She continues:

Mr. Illingworth says he never did demand a halfpenny; if they would give it well and good, if not, they let it alone. He sent the bellman about town first to desire folks would send for their letters, or else give the men a halfpenny for bringing them, which he says is a custom in a great many places, in some a penny. . . .

It will be seen from these extracts from the Byrom diaries that an arrangement for house delivery in a Post town which took the form of a paid service in 1764 was, in Manchester for certain, and by report elsewhere, an unofficial custom nearly twenty years earlier.

The first real official effort to provide a postal service for the villages was made in 1801. A fifth clause of an Act passed in that year authorised the Postmaster-General to make special arrangements with towns, villages, and hamlets off the Post routes for the conveyance and collection of their letters, a sum to be mutually agreed being charged for the service. The sum was either a penny or a halfpenny, depending on the distance entailed. There was a snag about the procedure in that the inhabitants of the village concerned had to find someone to guarantee to make up any losses incurred. Thus, a Fifth Clause Post, as it was called, might be inaugurated with great enthusiasm. In practice, the number of letters carried might be infinitesimal, so that the sum required to make up for the loss on running it might be considerable.

The Fifth Clause Posts became popular very slowly. Two years after the Act was passed, there were only thirteen of them, run at a total profit of £55 7s. This modest little figure did indicate, however, that the service could be made to pay if run on a large scale, and no doubt the profit motive influenced the authorities as much as their desire to foster the habit of letter-writing. The objects of these Fifth Clause Posts was officially described in 1804 as follows:

> Posts of this description are established with a view to bringing the correspondence of villages in the vicinity of Post towns under the control and direction of the Postmaster-General, and, by affording convenience, regularity, and responsibility in the delivery and collection of the letters, and by charging equitable and moderate prices over and above the postage to the Post town, to bring the inhabitants of such villages into the custom of writing solely by post, and perhaps a greater number of letters than they did before, so that if the amount of the extra pence should happen to do little more at first than cover the expenses of the first messenger and receiving houses, yet the general revenue is sure to be benefited, and a new establishment is made, which by time and circumstance generally becomes a source of profit also.

A typical example of the way in which the Fifth Clause Posts worked is that of the mid-Kent. It was set up in 1804 and took advantage of two Post towns so that a type of shuttle service could be maintained. Two postmen were employed, at a wage of 19s. a week each. One started out from Dartford and the other from Sevenoaks at 6 a.m. each morning. The Dartford man, who carried mail left by the London-Dover mail coach, walked through Sutton-at-Hone, Farningham, Otford, Shoreham, and Kemsing. There he met the man from Sevenoaks, who came via Wrotham. They exchanged bags and returned along their own routes. The point about this system was that not only did it bring letters posted from London the previous night deep into the heart of Kent, an area which is still very much off the beaten track, but it enabled a cross-Post to be run. People in Hastings, Battle, Tunbridge Wells, Tonbridge, and Sevenoaks could correspond with friends in the north Kent towns beyond Kemsing and down to the coast at Dover. It was a speedy route for such letters, which previously had to be sent on the coach to London and then sent out again. Instead of forty-eight hours for a letter from, say, Hastings to Dartford, anyone who liked to contact the postman by 6 a.m. knew that his letter would be in Dartford the same evening.

One legal factor crippled the expansion of the Fifth Clause Posts —and that was the necessity for the Post Office to carry franks and newspapers free of charge. There was no legal power to change this proviso in the case of the rural Posts, so that very often the postmen were trudging miles with letters and newspapers which did not bring a penny of revenue to the Post Office. As early as 1808 the Postmaster-General decided that the Fifth Clause Posts should only be set up for small towns, and that Penny Posts. which were technically unofficial and therefore not liable to the necessity for carrying franks and newspapers free, should be encouraged in the villages. Penny Posts immediately began to expand. By 1838 there were 1,922 villages in the United Kingdom served by them, while the Fifth Clause Posts had only reached a total of fifty-two.

Even so, there was little satisfaction in the state of the rural Posts. The figure of 1,922 villages is obviously small in relation to the number of parishes, and bears no comparison with the 24,000 post offices and sub-offices which exist to-day.

It was stated in 1838 with some truth that " an inspection of the Post Office maps will show that, even in England, where the ramifications of the Post Office distribution are more minute than in any other part of the Kingdom, there are districts considerably larger than the county of Middlesex into which the postman never enters ".

6

THE MAIL COACH ERA

IN the last half of the eighteenth century, stage coaches were running much faster than the Postboys who carried the mails. People who wanted a letter to reach a town quickly did not use the Posts. They paid a stage coachman to take it for them, and it would arrive at the coaching office hours or even days before the Post. Such letters had to be made up into parcels to avoid breaking the rules of the postal monopoly, and there naturally followed absurd discussions as to what constituted a parcel and what was legally a letter.

In their advertisements, the coach-owners discreetly stressed their parcel-carrying service, which everyone knew was a polite fiction for letters. Here is an announcement of 1767 which appeared in the *Sherborne, Shaftesbury and Dorchester Journal*:

THE PROPRIETORS OF THE
FROME STAGE-MACHINE,

In order to make it more agreeable to their Friends in the West, have engaged to set out Post Chaises from the Christopher Inn in Wells every Sunday, Tuesday, and Thursday evenings, at Five o'clock, to stop at the George Inn, at Shepton Mallett, and set out from thence at a quarter past six, to carry passengers and parcels to Frome, to be forwarded from thence to London in the One Day Flying Machine, which began on Sunday, April the 12th, 1767. Also a Chaise from Frome every Tuesday, Thursday, and Saturday evenings to Shepton and Wells as soon as the coach arrives from London.

Performed by
R. MESSETER, at the Crown, at Thatcham, and
J. HITCHCOCK, at the Catherine Wheel, Beckhampton.

John Palmer, a theatre proprietor of Bath, was the most fervent agitator for the establishment of coaches to carry the mails. His work necessitated many journeys to London and other towns in connection with the engagement of actors and playwrights for his theatre, and he quickly noticed that his coach constantly overtook the postboys on the Bath Road. The Post took fifty-two hours between Bath and London; the Diligence completed the journey in less than twenty hours. Palmer described the postboy of the day as an " idle boy mounted on a worn-out hack who, so far from being able to defend himself against a robber, was more likely in league with him ".

This was the era of the highwayman, a more romantic figure in retrospect than in actual experience, for his gallantry is rather a matter of fiction than a fact of history. Postboys were unarmed, they frequently carried valuables, and they were abroad at night. It is small wonder that the so-called gentlemen of the road found such people more likely victims than a well-filled and fast-moving coach. So universal was mail robbery at this time that the Post Office itself issued advice to those sending money or negotiable documents to cut them in half and send them by instalments. Palmer also wished to use soldiers as guards for the coaches. This suggestion did not prove practicable, though the arming of the guards who rode with the drivers did in effect provide similar protection, and it is significant that, with the advent of the mail coach, the general menace of the highwaymen largely disappeared from the roads. Clearly they had prowled the thickets and commons chiefly for the purpose of robbing the Post, and not on the off-chance that some passing passenger coach included a lady adorned with a fortune in jewellery.

Palmer's report concluded with the statement:

The Post at present, instead of being the swiftest, is almost the slowest conveyance in the country; and though, from the great improvement in our roads, other carriers have proportionately mended their speed, the Post is as slow as ever. Rewards have frequently been offered by Postmasters-General for the best constructed mail cart, or some plan to prevent the frequent robbery of the mail, but without effect.

Palmer had a benevolent friend in Pitt, who was (at the time when Palmer was putting forward his mail coach plans) Chancellor of the Exchequer in the Shelburne Ministry. Pitt, who spent a lot of time in Bath when his Government duties permitted, was enthusiastic about the scheme, but he was not able to see that it was carried out until he himself became Prime Minister.

The first mail coach ran on 2 August 1784 from Bristol to London. The advertisement which appeared in the *Bristol Journal* graphically describes the innovation.

The Diligence is constructed so as to accommodate four inside Passengers in the Most Convenient Manner. It will set off every night at eight o'clock from the Swan with Two Necks, Lad Lane, London, and arrive at the Three Tuns, Bath, before ten o'clock of the next morning, and at the Rummer Tavern, near the Exchange, Bristol, at Twelve. The Coach will depart from the said Tavern at Bristol at four o'clock every afternoon, and arrive in London at eight o'clock the next morning.

Both the Guards and the Coachmen (who will likewise be armed) have given ample security for their Conduct to the Proprietors, so that those Ladies and Gentlemen who may please to honour them with their encouragement may depend on every Respect and Attention.

The *Gentleman's Magazine* reported the historic event as follows:

Monday, August 2. Began a new plan for the conveyance of the Mail between London, Bath and Bristol, by coaches constructed for that purpose. The coach which left London this evening at 8 o'clock arrived at Bristol the next morning before 11; and the coach that set out from Bristol at 4 o'clock in the afternoon, got into London before 8 o'clock the next morning; and in this regular order the coaches have continued every day since.

The Bristol coach was always regarded as the senior coach in later years and on the mass departure of the mail coaches from St. Martin's le Grand it always headed the procession.   The

This letter, written in July 1653, bears in the centre the words " Haste, Haste, Post Haste ". On either side (vertically) can be seen the times of receipt at various stages of its journey. The letter concerned naval matters.

HENRY BISHOP

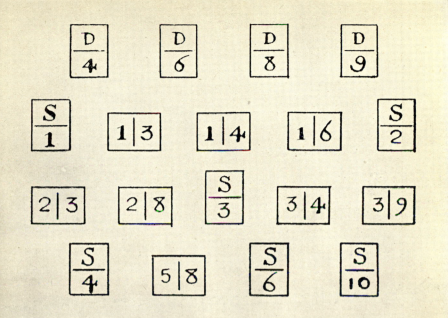

TOP: The first " postage due " stamps introduced in the Bishop system about 1663.
' D ' stands for pennies and ' S ' for shillings. BOTTOM: One of the earliest post-
marks known—17 May 1661. It is a Bishop mark, used to indicate time of delivery.
Note the charge of 3d.—bottom right.

Two letters sent through the London penny post after the Dockwra system was taken over by the Post Office. That on the left was sent in May, 1770, and the note on the right in 1729. Both have been marked " Penny Post Paid."

London-Bristol mail run was an outstanding success. Pitt immediately authorised extensions. By the spring of 1785 mail coaches were running to Norwich, and in the summer of that year to Leeds, Liverpool, and Manchester. By the time winter came, a Londoner could send a letter to Gloucester, Swansea, Birmingham, Oxford, Holyhead, Carlisle, Dover, and Exeter, as well as any town *en route*, by mail coach. In 1786 the last important route went over to mail coaches—the Great North Road to Scotland. The time between London and Edinburgh was shortened from eighty-five hours for the fastest Post horse to sixty hours by Diligence.

At no period of postal history has there been anything to capture the glamour and excitement of the mail coach. In the fifty years that the vehicle flourished and withered it caused a social revolution, not only because of the speed and ease of written communication that it brought, but on account of the way the very sight of it bound town and country, North and South, closer together. There was something very significant to the Scottish lowlander on his way to work to pause and watch the coach go by which he knew had been rumbling along the deserted streets of London town only sixty hours earlier. Its very speed was a dangerous and heady novelty for the old-fashioned, and it was with some daring that people entered the vehicle which would take them swaying through the night at a speed of as much as fifteen miles an hour at times. There were many stories of people who died from fright during such bursts of speed, and many a physician learnedly explained that the celerity would give rise to an affection of the brain. But to more sensible people the ability to travel about the kingdom in comparative comfort and with complete assurance that the journey would be completed on time meant a significant step forward in a broader and more intelligent interest in the affairs of one's fellows, those strangers who had once lived at impossible distances of 200 miles or more.

The size of the coaches varied. Some were pulled by two horses which were changed every six miles. At the other extreme were magnificent affairs drawn by a team of six, with a postilion on the leading outside horse. But eventually the happy medium of a coach-and-four became general.

The mail guard was the most imposing figure on the resplendent vehicle and its only Post Office official. His coat was of scarlet with blue lapels and white ruffles. The coat lining of blue matched the blue of the heavy cloth waistcoat. He wore nankeen breeches and white silk stockings, while the hat had a splendid gilt band. The curved bugle of Elizabethan days, though still used as the insignia of the Posts, had given way to a long brass horn on which the guard could play his own composition, so that every innkeeper, every stableboy, and every turnpike guard would know immediately who was in charge of the mail that day.

Despite his ostentation and spectacular dress, the coach guard was no mountebank. Even if drivers changed after a few stages, as they usually did, the guard often went right through except on the longest runs. On fine summer days it was doubtless a delightful experience to sit high above the road as the horses kept up their standard eight miles an hour, but after twelve hours of a bitter winter's night, with blinding sleet blackening the feeble glimmer of the lamps, it was no job for a weakling.

Furthermore, he was a guard, and had to be ready to defend the mail with his life. The mail was carried in a locked box at the rear on which the guard kept his feet. As he approached a Post town he opened the box and took out the bag of letters to be left at that destination. Then, a mile away, he blew long blasts on his horn. If the horses were not to be changed, the coach would not even slow up as it passed the Post-house. The driver would take the coach close to the house and the postman would be ready leaning out of the first-floor window. With a dexterous and simultaneous movement, the delivery bag would be flipped upwards and the outgoing bag thrown down towards the guard. If by any chance the postman was too sleepy to bestir himself the mail was taken on to the end of the run. Only in exceptional circumstances would the coach stop between stages for the delivery or collection of letters.

The guard's weapons were carried in a case which contained a cutlass, two pistols, and a blunderbuss. In the case of accident to the coach—and there were plenty of instances of overturning and collision through the breakneck driving along the narrow, unlit roads at night, it was his duty to unhitch a horse and ride on it with the mail to the next stage. Sometimes the coach became stuck in mud or snowdrifts. In that case the guard tried to force his mount through, and if he could not manage that he walked. There were many reports of great heroism on the part of guards who attempted impossible feats to see that the mail got through. At Christmas, 1836, a guard started out from the Birmingham-London coach, which had to be abandoned at Aylesbury, and, with the help of two postboys who had been waiting to put the mail on the coach, he rode through one of the worst blizzards ever recorded and succeeded in reaching London, thirty miles away. He brought the only mail to get through from the north-west and south-west for forty-eight hours.

Some years before this the Edinburgh mail coach became snow-bound at Moffat. The coachman and the guard mounted the horses and, with the company of two postboys, started across the bleak country to the next stage. The drifts were too deep for the horses, and they were sent back. The two men then set out alone, carrying the mail bags. On the following day the bags were found lashed to a post beside the road. The bodies were dug out of a snowdrift many days afterwards. In their failure, these two men, James MacGeorge and John Goodfellow, gained a high place on the roll of honour of many men and women who have sacrificed their lives to maintain the watchword of the Royal Mail: that the post must get through.

The mail coaches in their early years departed from the General Post Office in Lombard Street every week-night between 8 and 8.20 p.m. It was a great sight; and even more spectacular after the new G.P.O. was opened in 1829 in St. Martin's le Grand.

During the day the vehicles were greased, cleaned, and polished in the coachyard at Millbank, Westminster. Then, about five o'clock, two horses drew them slowly along the cobbled streets to various inns near the G.P.O. The Swan with Two Necks, in Lad Lane, a thoroughfare near Gresham Street which, like the inn, has since disappeared, was one of the most important. From its yard departed the mail coaches for Exeter, Bath and Devonport; Salisbury and Exeter; Exeter, Devonport, and Falmouth; Nottingham and Halifax; Birmingham, Shrewsbury, and Holyhead (for

Ireland); Peterborough, Lincoln, and Hull; Lichfield, Warrington, and Liverpool; Ipswich and Norwich; Bristol and Pembroke; Manchester, Carlisle and Port Patrick; Southampton and Poole; Cirencester and Stroud; Cambridge, King's Lynn, and Wells-next-the-Sea; and Dover.

From the Golden Cross at the Charing Cross end of the Strand mail coaches left for Gloucester and Carmarthen; Dover; Nottingham and Halifax; Hastings; Cirencester and Stroud. From the Bell and Crown, Holborn, the coaches took on passengers for Salisbury and Exeter; Boston and Louth; Cambridge, King's Lynn, and Wells-next-the-Sea. At the Spread Eagle, Gracechurch Street, the routes covered were Exeter, Devonport, and Falmouth; and Peterborough, Lincoln and Hull. At Blossom's Inn, Lawrence Lane, stood the Brighton coach. At the Bull and Mouth, St. Martin's Lane, Wetherby, Carlisle, and Glasgow; Nottingham, Sheffield, and Leeds; Worcester and Ludlow; Exeter, Falmouth, and Penzance; Edinburgh and Thurso. From the Saracen's Head, Snow Hill, the coach for Boston and Louth. From the White Horse, Fetter Lane, Portsmouth; and Ipswich and Yarmouth. From the Belle Sauvage, Ludgate Hill, Newmarket and Norwich; and from the Bolt-in-Tun, Fleet Street, Portsmouth and Hastings.

In the yards of these inns the four horses to take the coach on its first stage were harnessed, while the luggage was stowed on board and the passengers settled down for their long journey through the night. The scenes must have been as bustling and exciting as anything at a modern railway terminus, and the onlooker at the Swan with Two Necks must have marvelled at the fact that within this single yard travellers could step aboard a vehicle which would take them to the four corners of the country—to Ipswich or Falmouth, Holyhead or Leeds. Eight coaches all due to leave simultaneously to take up their position in a single file outside the G.P.O. was a sight that Londoners loved to see, and was a matter of wide-eyed wonder to the rural traveller on his first visit to the Metropolis.

There are vivid pictures of coach travel in many of Dickens's books, and none better than those in *Nicholas Nickleby*. Here, for instance, is the scene as a coach left on the first stage of its long journey to Yorkshire:

" Sit fast here, gentlemen," said the guard as he clambered up.

" All right behind there, Dick? " cried the coachman.

" All right," was the reply. " Off she goes! " And off she did go—if coaches be feminine—amidst a loud flourish from the guard's horn, and the calm approval of all the judges of coaches and coach-horses congregated at the Peacock, but more especially of the helpers, who stood, with the cloths over their arms, watching the coach till it disappeared, and then lounged admiringly stablewards, bestowing various gruff encomiums on the beauty of the turnout.

When the guard (who was a stout old Yorkshireman) had blown himself quite out of breath, he put the horn into a little tunnel of a basket fastened to the coach side for the purpose, and giving himself a plentiful shower of blows on the chest and shoulders, observed it was uncommon cold; after which, he demanded of every person separately whether he was going right through, and if not where he was going. Satisfactory replies being made to those queries, he surmised that the roads were pretty heavy after the fall last night, and took the liberty of asking whether any of the gentlemen carried a snuff-box. It happened that nobody did, he remarked with a mysterious air that he had heard a medical gentleman as went down to Grantham last week, say how that snuff-taking was bad for the eyes; but for his part he had never found it so, and what he said was that everybody should speak as they found. Nobody attempted to controvert this position; he took a small brown paper parcel out of his hat, and putting on a pair of horn spectacles (the writing being crabbed) read the direction half-a-dozen times over; having done which, he consigned the parcel to its old place, put up his spectacles again, and stared at everybody in turn. After this, he took another blow at the horn by way of refreshment; and, having now exhausted his usual topics of conversation, folded his arms as well as he could in so many coats, and falling into a solemn silence, looked carelessly at the familiar objects which met his eye on every side as the coach rolled on; the only things he seemed to care for being horses and droves of cattle, which he scrutinised with a critical air as they were passed on the road.

And for a cameo of the arrival of a coach in London there is this description of the Metropolis as seen by the Yorkshireman John Brodie and his bride:

The night, fraught with so much bitterness for one poor soul, had given place to a bright and cloudless summer morning, when a North-country mail-coach traversed, with cheerful noise, the yet silent streets of Islington, and giving brisk note of its approach with the lively winding of the guard's horn, clattered onward to its halting-place hard by the Post-office.

The only outside passenger was a burly, honest-looking countryman on the box, who, with his eyes fixed upon the dome of St. Paul's Cathedral, appeared so wrapt in admiring wonder, as to be quite insensible to all the bustle of getting out the bags and parcels, until one of the coach windows being let sharply down, he looked round, and encountered a pretty female face which was just then thrust out.

"See there, lass!" bawled the countryman, pointing towards the object of his admiration, "There be Paul's Church. 'Ecod, he be a soizable 'un, he be."

"Goodness, John! I shouldn't have thought it could have been half the size. What a monster!"

"Monsther!—Ye're aboot right theer, I reckon, Mrs. Browdie," said the countryman good-humouredly, as he came slowly down in his huge top-coat, "and wa'at dost thee tak' yon place to be noo—thot 'un ower the wa'. Ye'd never coom near it 'gin ye thried for twolve moonths. It's na' but a Poast-office! Ho! Ho! They need to charge for dooble latthers. A Poast-office! Wa'at dost thee think o' thot? 'Ecod, if thot's on'y a Poast-office, I'd loike to see where the Lord Mayor o' Lunnun lives."

So crowded were the roads around the Post Office when the procession of as many as thirty mail coaches was lined up, the mail safely in the boot and the horses tossing their heads

impatiently for what they knew from experience was the start, that
regulations were passed forbidding hackney carriages to stand in
the vicinity, and hawkers were not allowed to display their wares
or loiter on the pavement. Although the congestion of mail traffic
has long since disappeared into the great yard of Mount Pleasant
these regulations still exist.

The mail coaches were all of the same design, and painted in
maroon and black. They were built in the Millbank yard by
Vidler, a junior partner to a man named Besant, who had
received the first contracts for building mail coaches in 1787 from
Palmer. Vidler made a considerable fortune from the monopoly
he held, for he never sold his coaches to the contractors who ran
the Post routes, but merely hired them on a mileage basis. The
London-Bristol coach, for example, brought him about £14 a week,
and with twenty-seven coaches running anything from fifty miles
to Dover to six hundred on the Thurso run, it can be realised that
the revenue was large, even though the vehicles were driven hard
in fair weather and foul and had to be constantly repaired and
replaced. There was so much criticism of this monopoly that in
1836 the contract was auctioned publicly and Vidler excluded from
the bidding. It does not appear that he made much of a protest
about this, and after twenty-five years of lucrative business he
could well afford to watch someone else incur the risks of loss
which would occur if the coaches faded from the scene in the face
of railway competition, as, of course, they soon did.

Vidler did not supply coaching horses. They came from the
contractors who maintained the routes, and their stables were
strung out all along the road, very few of them organising relief
teams for more than fifty miles from their own towns. The
majority of these contractors ran ordinary passenger stage coaches
as well as the mails, and built up very large businesses. At the
Swan with Two Necks there were stables for 200 horses; down at
the Hounslow stage the same proprietor kept another 150 animals
at the Crown and Cushion Tavern.

The principal coaches had names. There was the Tally Ho on
the London-Birmingham run, the Comet which ran to Southampton, and the Manchester Defiance. Another coach on the Manchester run was called the Telegraph, and this synonym of speed

was also the name for the London-Exeter mail.   Lovers of Dickens
will recall the hilarious description of Pickwick's Christmas ride
to Dingley Dell on the Muggleton Telegraph.

It was reckoned too, that to provide an efficient service a horse
for every mile of the route had to be provided.   Thus on the 185-
mile run to Manchester 185 horses had to be maintained, housed,
and fed to keep the seventeen changes running smoothly.   This
figure seems large, but it will be realised that a group of four
animals which had completed a gruelling run of ten or a dozen
miles from London on a winter's night had to be rested and could
not be expected to take the inward-bound coach back to their own
stables a few hours later.   Incidentally, the change of horses took
place in under two minutes at efficient posts.

The coaching inns which are still to be seen on the trunk roads
of Britain were on the average busier in those days than they are
even in this era of motors. Nowadays the landlord and his servants
can go to bed long before midnight, and the road will be comparatively quiet except for the rumbling lorries and an occasional
fast-travelling private motor car.   In winter there will be long
periods when the road is utterly deserted.   But at the zenith of the
mail coach era this yard was a hive of activity day and night in
both winter and summer and whatever the weather.   On the Great
North Road coaches were passing any spot south of Ware at
intervals of twenty minutes day and night, and woe betide the
reputation of any innkeeper who could not serve a massive meal
of several courses at two or three in the morning to a group of
famished and wearied coach passengers.   He knew to the minute
the time the coach would arrive if his inn was a stage.   The mail
guards on the coaches carried a sealed watch and a timetable which
was handed on from one to the other.   It gave the precise schedule
for the journey, and it was the mail guard's task to see that any
delay in starting was made up during the journey to the next
stage.   Some indication of this exact timing, which would do
credit to many a suburban electric train to-day, can be seen from
the old waybills issued for the information of passengers.   At
Wetherby, for instance, the London-Glasgow passengers are
warned that they have exactly thirty-five minutes for dinner—
from 4.36 p.m. to 5.11 p.m.   On another bill the arrival time of

the Bath coach from London is given as 6.32 a.m., and at exactly this time it pulled into the yard of the Three Tuns and changed its horses for the final stage to Bristol. No wonder that the lives of people all along these routes were organised by the passing of the coaches, and those that had clocks would often adjust them sooner than believe that the coach was wrong! Post Office time became a standard, as it still is through " TIM " to-day.

On the busier routes, under the spur of competition, this regard for precise time-keeping reached almost bizarre heights. On the London-Brighton run, where four services competed, times were actually given to the half-minute. Barmaids rushed out with trays of drinks at the stages. There was no time to get out. On one of the West-Country services local charities received 8d. from the proud proprietor for every minute the coaches were behind time.

Although fares were cut by the stage coaches, which invariably ran in opposition to the mail coaches on the same route, the latter always winning in this form of cut-throat competition because of their freedom from tolls and greater reliability, travelling on the mail stages was something of a luxury even by to-day's standards of the value of the £1. The posting inns were much superior to the ordinary inns, and if the meals were good they were very expensive. Dinner was 6s. with compulsory extras, such as 2s. for candles and 7s. for a bottle of wine. Some of the innkeepers were supposed to be in league with the coachmen, so that the post-horn sounded almost as soon as the travellers had reached the third of the five courses which dinner usually comprised. The food was then taken away, ready for the arrival of the coach from the other direction.

Rivalry between the coaches was responsible for accidents, and it is significant of the breakneck speed that they were driven that a minute issued by the Post Office advised people not to send coins through the post, "partly from the prejudice it does the coin by the friction it occasions from the great expedition with which it is conveyed, and especially as the cash is likely to fall out of the letter through jolting".

People to-day who shake their heads at the activities of the roadhogs would have had much to complain about more than a century ago, and a newspaper report like the following invariably aroused a lot of heated correspondence from indignant readers who bewailed the end of the leisurely days of yore. It appeared in the *Liverpool Mercury* dated 4 April 1823:

STAGE COACH ACCIDENT

The dangerous and highly culpable system of racing, which has so long and so justly [been] complained of by all persons who have had occasion to travel on the road between Liverpool and Carlisle, may, perhaps, meet a check from the circumstances we have this week to relate. On Monday last, two of these coaches, the Robert Burns and the North Briton, were coming at their accustomed speed towards Preston from Liverpool striving for the lead, when the former was upset on Penwortham Bridge, and the driver and three outside passengers falling against the battlement were dreadfully cut and mangled. In coming down Penwortham Hill, the North Briton was first, but before they reached the bridge the Robert Burns passed its opponent. In rising the bridge, however, the horses of the other coach came abreast of the Robert Burns which caused the driver to give additional impulse to his team. Having at this time to make a sudden turn the coach lost its equilibrium, and came down on the right side with great force. One passenger's leg was laid open from the foot to the knee. The driver and other passengers were dreadfully mangled about the head.

Perhaps the passage of time may help us to forgive the foolhardy risks that caused such disasters as this and to remember only the excitement and thrills which such driving must have brought to the onlookers. In those days townsfolk were every bit as proud of their own mail coach as their descendants are of the local football team, and no doubt in the case cited above the coaches were symbols of rivalry between two towns, with the drivers striving for the honour of their own birthplaces.

Possibly it is better to remember the mail coach skimming along on the fine morning of a day when history was made. Nelson's great victories of Camperdown, the Nile, Trafalgar, the victory of Waterloo, the passing of the first Reform Bill—such events were the occasion for coaches to be decorated with oak leaves and laurels, and the horses would have ribbons streaming from the reins and flowers tied to the harness. The guard would give an extra flourish to his post horn call, and as the coaches rolled by the good tidings would be shouted to the labourers in the fields, the women streaming from the village cottages. Coachman and passengers alike would shout the news, so that it spread far and wide in the wake of the mails, reaching farther and farther into the provinces of England, into Wales and the fastness of the northern Scottish Highlands, as the day wore on.

Apart from these historic occasions, there were traditional days when the mail coaches were decorated. At Christmas both vehicle and team were festooned with sprigs of holly and ribbons, and the coachman and guard wore sprigs of mistletoe. On May Day, too, flowers and evergreens were entwined everywhere. In addition to being part of the traditional festival of spring of Merrie England, these May Day decorations were also symbolic of the return of the coach to its regular route, most of them having been withdrawn during the winter until the mail contracts were given. 1 May had been the day when the service was resumed.

To travel by mail on that spring morning must have been an experience indeed, and it was the sole occasion of the year when the strict time-table was allowed to lapse, at least so far as the stages run in daylight were concerned. At each town the coaches were held up by the inhabitants, and the prettiest girls brought glasses of cider and beer, with confectionery and cakes, for the coachman, guard, and passengers. In some places — notably Sutton-on-Trent, a stage on the Great North Road—this ceremony of holding up the mail coach lasted for the whole of the first week of May, and so much food was provided by the inhabitants that the inn did not supply meals for the travellers.

In the last months of the mail coach era the average speed of all the main coach lines was maintained at a minimum of ten miles an hour. The time-tables of some of the principal lines are worth noting for comparison with modern methods of transportation:

London-Edinburgh (400 miles) . .	45½ hours
London-York (197 miles) . . .	20 hours
London-Manchester (185 miles) . .	19 hours
London-Exeter (176 miles) . . .	19 hours
London-Holyhead (259 miles) . .	27 hours
London-Devonport (216 miles) . .	21 hours

At the end of 1830, the monopoly of the mail coaches was broken with the first mail despatch by rail. They died even more quickly than they had risen after Pitt's authorisation came through. The mail coaches of the Bath Road, the pioneer service of them all, ceased running in June 1841, when Brunel's Great Western Railway was opened from Paddington to Bristol. The last of the old London mail coaches pulled into London on 6 January 1848. It came from Norwich and Newmarket. There is no record that there was any ceremony or special recognition for the coachman, the guard, and his faithful team as they brought an era to an end in the half-light of that winter's morning. But elsewhere the final run saw crowds in tears as civic dignitaries bade the coach goodbye instead of *au revoir*. At Newcastle, for example, when the last coach for Edinburgh went on its way in 1847, flags were at half-mast. But there were still remote areas of the British Isles where the iron horse had not yet come, and the mail coach, maybe a shadow of its former glory in sparkling paint and gleaming brasswork on the crack runs from London, still lurched and swayed along the lanes and stony tracks to see that the mail came to Her Majesty's subjects. They remained in operation in Ireland and Scotland for many years. The last one, to Thurso in the northern Highlands of Scotland, was still in operation in 1874.

7

ROYAL MAIL BY RAIL

NOVEMBER 11 1830 was a momentous day in the history of the Royal Mail. On that day the first pouch of letters went by railway train from Liverpool to Manchester. The average speed of the trains at that time was twenty miles an hour, so that the new system almost halved the time taken by the coach mails. The number of letters between the two towns rapidly increased, and after a contract for the regular carriage of mails by rail was signed in the following year four despatches a day were arranged.

The comparatively short distance of this first railway mail did not unduly disturb the protagonists of the mail coach, but in 1837 there came a development which was, in less than a decade, to destroy the intricate system of road communications which had been so quickly built up. In the summer of that year the Grand Junction Railway from Birmingham was joined to the Manchester-Liverpool system, providing more than seventy miles of rail system. On 3 July a mail was conveyed from London to Liverpool in sixteen and a half hours. It went by mail coach to Birmingham, and was there put on the railway.

On the Birmingham-Liverpool run the actual horse-drawn coach was mounted bodily on a flat truck for the rail section of the journey. When special mail coaches were built for railway use, the design followed the road version almost identically, even to the guard's seat on the outside. The unfortunate man rode there to protect the mails just as he had done on the King's highway.

Very soon the railway link was not confined merely to letters for Liverpool and Manchester. It was used to speed up the Irish Posts as well. By these means a special fast mail for Dublin left London at 8 a.m. and reached Holyhead by 9.30 a.m. the next morning. Many mail coaches were taken off as a result of this development. The Liverpool and Manchester coaches all terminated at Birmingham, and the Holyhead coach, running via Shrewsbury, could not compete with the combined road-and-rail system. The following year saw a further victory by steam over the horse. On 20 September 1838 the line from London to Birmingham was opened, and the mail could go the entire journey of 200 miles to Liverpool by rail.

This was the great era of railway building in Britain. As the gangs of hundreds, and sometimes thousands, of labourers pushed their cuttings and embankments across the length and breadth of England, the Post Office changed their contracts from road to the new system as soon as trains were running. Like most modern developments, the facilities offered by the use of the railways necessitated increased Post Office expenditure long before results could be obtained. This fact, plus a growing abuse by the users, brought to a head the whole question of the franking system. The idea of allowing privileged persons to send mail free had been one of the proposals put forward during the Cromwell régime. It was then stated that '' Letters of all members of the legislative power are to be carried free from postage, and endorsement made indicating that they are for the service of the Commonwealth ''.

This meant that any senior Government official or M.P. simply signed the cover of the letter and it went forward free. On the face of it, the idea was reasonable, for there was little justification for one section of the Government paying the other for its services. But the frank, as the signature endorsement came to be known. was quickly exploited. The Postmasters themselves were regarded as Government officials and allowed to sign letters. Some of them had correspondence addressed to them, which was then forwarded privately for a special fee. Government officials signed covers by the score for their friends. By 1714 the Post Office was spending £25,000 a year to convey these free letters. Protests were made by the authorities at intervals, and in 1764 an Act was passed in an attempt to curb the practice. For the first time there were severe penalties for the forgery of the signature—up to seven years' transportation. This Act admittedly stopped the gravest abuses when they were felonious, but did little to restrict the tolerant attitude of Government officials on their own right to frank letters to friends and relations. This was a human failing which was bound to continue while the principle of such a privilege existed. An M.P. would frank his letter to his son at school; naturally, Mother's letter was also included. Next time Mother wrote by herself, at the same time writing half a dozen replies awaited by various friends and relations. What husband could refuse to frank these too? After all, they probably included a message of goodwill from him, so they were really his letters! Then Great Aunt Anne, staying at the M.P.'s home for the summer, wrote a lot of letters. These were also franked by her host. So it went on, among the nonentities as well as the famous. Horace Walpole franked his friends' letters by the hundred. Samuel Johnson went to great trouble to find an acquaintance with a frank so that a shilling or two could be saved. Kindly landlords provided them for their tenants, and less kindly masters paid their servants' wages with parcels of franks which had to be hawked from house to house. These covers were treasured by their owners and used again and again.

Palmer, the man who organised the mail coach services, put forward the sensible suggestion that those having the franking privilege should also include the date under the signature to prevent this re-use of the covers and to restrict mass production of franks to give friends a supply lasting several months. It was adopted in the Act of 1784, with rulings that the cover must include signature, date, town of origin and address of recipient, all in the same handwriting. That some officials did not object to increased clerical work in order to provide their friends with franking facilities is indicative either of a remarkable sense of friendship or else that some of the minor lights were doing the job for a fee. Regrettably, the latter seems more likely, for some M.Ps. franking letters on behalf of commercial interests were earning an income of several hundreds a year by an hour or so's work a week in the firms' correspondence departments before mail day.

It was estimated that when the Act came into force the number of franks being handled by the Post Office was 800,000 a year. Ten years later things were worse than ever. A census of franks indicated that Members of the House of Commons with business interests were writing so-called personal and official letters at the rate of 27,000 a year. Their colleagues who happened to be on the boards of the many banks then opening showed a similar facility with the pen. They franked more than 30,000 covers a month. Even the punishment of transportation did not frighten the forgers. One man counterfeited M.P.s' signatures on 12,000 covers and made a very good living out of it.

The franking system came to an end with the arrival of the Penny Post. Just before this historic step was made, five million franks a year were being handled by the Post Office. The payment on these letters was one of the reasons why Rowland Hill felt confident that cheaper postage rates would not necessarily result in the losses that the critics of his system feared. Certainly the loss of £500,000 on franks between 1716 and 1733 which was mentioned in the House of Commons in 1735 was a minor sum compared with losses at the beginning of the Railway Age.

The rates of postage in 1839, just before the reductions suggested by Rowland Hill, had remained unaltered since 1812. They were both involved and expensive. Remembering the greater value of money in those days it was obviously a matter for some forethought for ordinary folk to consider the despatch of a letter except for urgent personal or business reasons.

For a single letter the charges were:

Not exceeding 15 miles . .	4d.
15-20 miles	5d.
20-30 miles	6d.
30-50 miles	7d.
50-80 miles	8d.
80-120 miles	9d.
120-170 miles	10d.
170-230 miles	11d.
230-300 miles	1s.
300-400 miles	1s. 1d.
Over 400 miles . . .	1d.

for every additional 100 miles
There were other extra charges. A letter carried over the border

RALPH ALLEN

The Post Boy of the 1770's. It was his easy-going attitude and dilatory method which encouraged the development of the mail coach.

The courtyard of the old General Post Office in Lombard Street in the middle of the 18th century.

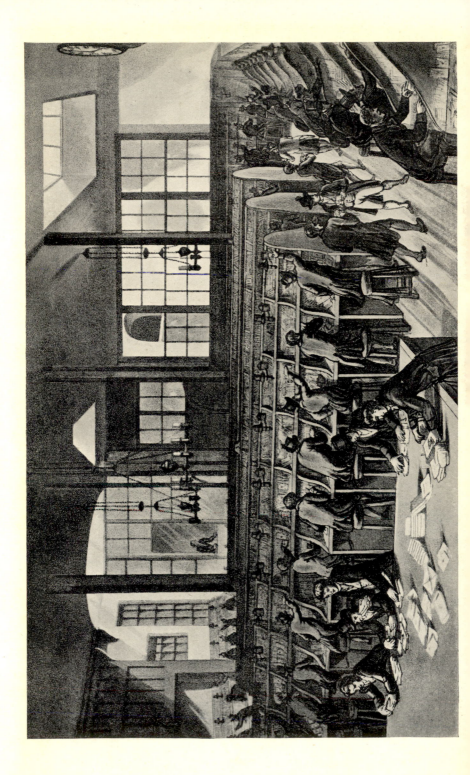

of Scotland by mail carriage with more than two wheels and for the sea section to Ireland via the Menai Bridge carried surcharges. Nor could much be sent in a letter. If it weighed as much as an ounce it counted as four letters. In addition there were various local postal charges. In London, if not on the G.P.O. delivery schedule, the charge was 2*d*. for addresses within three miles of the General Post Office, with a 3*d*. rate for addresses between three and twelve miles.

The harrowing stories of mothers pawning their clothes in order to pay the charges on a letter from an absent son may have been exaggerations, but it was certainly true that letter-writing when Queen Victoria came to the throne was a luxury. That was very soon to be changed.

3

8

AGITATION FOR THE
PENNY POST

Before 1839 the recurring changes in the rates of postage were rather similar, as regards their interest to the public, to the Budget alterations in the rates of income tax of the present time; there was often a revision, and almost as often it was bad news of an increase, tempered with a few concessions as regards anomalies on specific points.

The Post Office Act of 1711 fixed the rates of a period of thirty-two years. They were, in fact, retained until 1765, when some minor reductions were made on short-distance letters. In 1784, when Palmer's plan for using mail coaches came into operation, they were raised. This increase was typical of the temptations which any Chancellor of the Exchequer inevitably experiences when he is preparing his Budget. The revenue of the Post Office is so healthy, and derived from such tiny units of payment by the public, that there is a natural tendency to consider further tapping of this rich source of revenue, thereby changing the ideal of a letter rate fixed so as to cover the Post Office costs to a compromise of raising the nation's revenue.

The 1784 increases, which might have prejudiced the success of the mail coach innovation, were ordered by Pitt in place of a tax on coals which, as Chancellor of the Exchequer, he had proposed in his Budget Speech. The idea had been violently opposed in Parliament and was withdrawn. Just as had occurred when Charles II mulcted the postal revenues for more and more money with the rental charges soaring ever higher, even this extra burden imposed by Pitt did not proportionately slow the growth of the volume of letters. Pitt estimated his gains from postal rate

66

tax on the previous year's receipts of £159,000.   Thereafter they increased rapidly, so that by 1800 they had reached £720,000. When the war between Britain and France broke out, the Exchequer ordered increase after increase.   The rates were changed, always to a higher overall figure, in 1797, 1801, 1805, and 1812.

During the fifty years before the historic innovation of the Penny Post arrived in 1840, the increased rates were by no means the only burden restricting the potential developments of the Royal Mail.   The frank letters by 1793 were accounting for 900,000 pieces of mail a year.   Newspapers, then heavily taxed, also went free of charge.   This privilege added a further 9,000,000 pieces to be carried annually.   One may well conjecture the effects of the weight and volume which even the small-sized news sheets of the late eighteenth century must have had on the bag handed to the coach guard, and undoubtedly on many runs there were more newspapers and franks than anything else, an uneconomic practice which once again adds to one's surprise that the profits were maintained despite these burdens.

The 1797 increases in postage rates raised the cost of a letter going less than fifteen miles to 3d., and one from London to Edinburgh to 8d.   Intermediate rates went up in most cases by 1d. over the old charges.   There does not seem to have been a great outcry about it either by Parliament or the public.   It was, of course, a wartime measure, and the country showed its traditionally realistic appreciation of the necessity to pay for a war. In any case, the postage increases were only a single item of many pieces of bad news given to the tax-payer by Pitt.   There were increases or innovations of duty and tax on a variety of things, from snuff to tobacco, and from alcoholic drinks to iron.

Francis Freeling was the Post Office Secretary at this period. He had taken over the position in 1797.   He seems to have been thoroughly in favour of squeezing every penny out of the public that could be obtained without decreasing the volume of letters. On a narrow view, he may be criticised as a poor Post official for this reason; on the broader one, it was possibly a statesmanlike move in a time of war.   Whatever the motive, Freeling himself suggested the alterations which were passed into law in 1801. They were technical changes which, on the face of it, made no increase. In detail they altered the grouping of mileages on which the rates were based, so that long-distance letters paid more, increasing the cost of a letter in the extreme case of a journey from London to Edinburgh by 50 per cent. Distance from London became even more important than the name of the town concerned, and the postmarks of that time always included the distance from London. York is marked as 196, Nottingham as 127, the unit figure putting the correspondent into a higher category of postal payment.

The story of increases continues alongside the history of the prolonged wars with Napoleon. Another 1d. went on letters in 1805, and still another 1d. seven years later. Writing a letter which was to be sent any considerable distance was by now a luxury, and for ordinary folk something which only urgency would justify. It must be remembered that, apart from local Posts, the charges were at this time usually paid by the recipient. For a member of the working class to be confronted with a charge of 1s. or more must indeed have been a financial crisis. The sum was equivalent to a day's pay of many agricultural labourers at that time. It is small wonder that the Post Office had thousands of letters refused simply because the addressee could not, or would not, pay the charges. Many such cases are not so tragic as they might now appear. A Yorkshire lad going to seek his fortune in London would tell his parents that regularly every month he would send a letter to let them know that he was alive and well. He simply posted a blank sheet of paper with his parents' name and address on it. The parents would see the familiar handwriting of their son, know that he was alive and well, and refuse to accept the letter. They could not, of course, be forced to pay, and the Post Office had no redress from the sender as there were no details of his identity.

Pre-arranged codes in the address, by a mis-spelling or inclusion of an extra Christian name, would amplify the news, and in these cases an occasional letter paid for (the clue that this was to be accepted would be given on the cover) would itemise the codes for future messages for a period of several months. Such were the free postal methods for simple folk. Influential persons could usually find someone with a franking privilege. Dishonest people could buy franks, genuine or forged, or follow another common practice of including a letter inside a newspaper or writing the message in the margins. There can be no compromise over the illegality of such methods rife throughout the country at the time, but at least we can realise that the exorbitant rates imposed as a means of taxation were mainly to blame for the universal dishonesty.

There was just one increase in costs that might have raised charges, even the English rates, still further which the Post Office was able to avoid at this time, and that was the imposition of tolls on the mail coaches by the turnpike trusts. At the time of this agitation by the powerful interests behind the turnpikes, virtually every important road in the country was subject to toll, and if they had had their way rates of postage would have gone up to a prohibitive figure over long distances.

In order to speed up the mails, Palmer had suggested that his mail coaches should be free from tolls. The Post horses already passed the gates on the turnpikes without charge. In 1766 and 1773 two Acts of Parliament had made it legal to exact rates for the upkeep of roads instead of demanding compulsory labour from the local inhabitants. This seemed a sensible move, but in practice it further aggravated the public's disinclination to pay for the maintenance of the King's highway. Local inhabitants on the Great North Road, for example, saw no reason why they should contribute to the upkeep of a road used mainly by enormous wagons hauling goods from places many miles away to destinations just as remote.

Long before this, the turnpikes were causing bitter resentment among the common people. There were sporadic riots over many years. They broke out in 1728 and 1736, and again in the West Country in 1749, when gates near Bedminster and Bristol were destroyed. The biggest and best organised riot was that of 1753, when along the North Road dozens of turnpikes were destroyed in Yorkshire, virtually all the fit men of such towns as Otley and Yeadon turning out at midnight for the work of smashing the gates.

Succeeding Acts permitted the power of the turnpike trusts to be extended so that they could each maintain a reasonable length of road and exact charges from the users of it. Although there were exceptions, the turnpike trusts on the whole did an enormous amount of good to British roads, and they provided a decent surface to thoroughfares which had been little more than muddy tracks for centuries. The improvement alone made the use of the mail coach possible.

Before the era of the mail coaches came to a close, the number of turnpike trusts in England and Wales exceeded 1,100, and they were earning £1,800,000 a year from tolls. More than £1,000,000 of this was spent directly on road improvements, and the usefulness of the much-maligned trusts became evident as the roads quickly began to revert to their previous bad state once they were abolished. But by that time canals and railways were carrying the nation's fast traffic and heavy goods, and no one really cared, except the great taverns, which had thrived on the heyday of the King's highway and would have to wait nearly a hundred years for the internal combustion engine to make history repeat itself.

It was estimated that the turnpike trusts lost £50,000 a year because of the exemption of the 200 mail coaches from payment of tolls except for the passengers they carried. The trusts did not succeed in their plea for payment, except in Scotland, where exemption was restricted to coaches with two wheels. As all the mail coaches from London had four, these had to pay, and this meant another $\frac{1}{2}d$. on London letters to and from Scotland.

With the victory of Waterloo in 1815 there was a chance of relaxing taxation. The Post Office, while not getting any reductions on its payments to the Exchequer, was at least left alone. Thus, for a period of twenty-six years, the rates remained stable. They were, however, very involved, and the correspondence clerk in a London business house had to be a real expert on geography and regulations. The basic rates for distance ranged from 4d. for less than fifteen miles to 1s. 1d. on a distance of 300 to 400 miles. He had to check whether the town was across the Scottish border and therefore due for the $\frac{1}{2}d$. toll supplement. For Ireland he could choose between the 2d. rate across the sea via Holyhead or the faster road-rail route to Liverpool, which, however, meant an 8d. sea charge. A letter crossing the Menai Straits Bridge was charged 1d. extra, and if any letter weighed as much as an ounce it counted as four mailing pieces. He could

send the local letters for 2d. within a three-mile radius from the
General Post Office in Lombard Street; beyond that he had to
check up that it was within twelve miles, so that it could go for
3d., or just over that distance and therefore chargeable at 4d.

The tide of criticism was now rising. Robert Wallace, M.P. for
Greenock, was the most able and persistent questioner about the
Post Office in the House of Commons. The nominal head of the
Post Office at the time was the Earl of Lichfield, in the position
of Postmaster-General, but he was almost a figurehead, and the
real director was Sir Francis Freeling, the Secretary for the past
thirty years.

The information that Wallace gave the House was indeed reason
for disquiet. Freeling's salary was a nominal £500, and an actual
£4,600. He had created a job as Assistant Secretary for his son
at £800. Neither Freeling nor the Postmaster-General seemed to
spend a great amount of time at their desks. Wallace wanted to
have a board of management, and he would have achieved this
but for the House of Lords, where not unnaturally the several
members who had held the office of Postmaster-General for a few
months threw the Bill out. But this was by no means the end.
A Commission of Enquiry had been appointed, and although it
did not issue any report commensurate with the violent views of
Wallace, it did urge that reform was needed.

Freeling, an embittered old man, died the following year. His
final words show that he was not undeserving of sympathy in his
attitude to reduction in charges, even if his personal feathering
of his nest cannot be condoned. He mentioned how every
Chancellor of the Exchequer during his long career had nagged
him about the importance of maintaining the revenue, and he was
responsible in seeing that the money was forthcoming.

In 1837 five statutes replaced more than a hundred confusing
and redundant Acts relating to the Post Office which had been
passed in the previous three centuries. They brought some order
out of chaos, though they did little to reform the actual running
of the postal services. Something far less imposing than the long
legal sentences of a statute was to do that: a modest little
pamphlet, entitled *Post Office Reform: Its Importance and*

Practicability, by Rowland Hill. (Privately printed by W. Clowes & Sons, Stamford Street, 1837.)

Rowland Hill was a Radical. He was born in Kidderminster in 1795, the son of a schoolmaster, and by the time he was twelve he was teaching a class there himself. This does not quite indicate the brilliance one might imagine, for it was a common method of those days for children to teach one another. The delighted discoverer of this method of tuition described it as " an invention, under divine Providence, of a new and mechanical system of education, by which one master might conduct a school of 1,000 children with perfect ease ". The youngsters chosen as teachers simply repeated, parrot fashion, the words of the master to a group of children, who learned them by heart.

It is doubtful whether young Rowland had to follow quite as crude a method as this. The Hill family of six boys and two girls were brilliant children of a brilliant father and mother, though the father's idealism about education was not of a practical variety, and he was usually in financial straits. However, the school seems in latter years to have prospered fairly well and a second establishment was opened at Tottenham, where Rowland Hill came. Interested in anything that concerned progress and the common good, Rowland Hill began to study the criticisms in Parliament about the state of the Post Office, and through this became acquainted with Robert Wallace, the crusading M.P. Hill asked for all the published material that Wallace could lend him, so that he could study the whole business of the Posts. Wallace promptly despatched a cabful of statutes, reports, official papers, pamphlets, and histories. From a study of these emerged the historic pamphlet on postal reform, and it is no discredit to Rowland Hill to suggest the contents were not entirely his own work. With his brothers, he formed what in these days would be called a brains trust for the discussion of every personal and general problem which they desired to solve—a method of working out difficulties which was continued while they lived. The intellectual riches available were by this time great indeed. Mathew Hill was a great lawyer, Frederic wrote authoritative books on education, Edwin was an inventor, and the others were equally distinguished in their own sphere of interest.

Rowland Hill's pamphlet started by pointing out that, even though the return of peace had brought a Budget surplus, the wartime increases on the postage rates had not been reduced. He quoted figures to show that the rapid increase in population—a population much more literate than ever before—had not brought a corresponding increase in postal revenue. In other words, the Posts were not prospering.

The publication of a pamphlet was a popular method of those days for airing grievances and for putting forward any crank's particular fad. The contents were usually fiery and extreme in style, with a paucity of factual material to support their bizarre contentions. Not so Rowland Hill's. He adopted statistical methods similar to those of the sample surveys used to-day for the assessment of national facts and trends. He could not, for instance, find out the actual numbers of letters handled by the Post Office, as no such figures were kept. By careful calculation, however, in which details of the number of franked letters and the number of newspapers passing through the mails without charge were taken into account, he was able to arrive at a figure of $1\frac{1}{3}d$. as the average cost of distribution of a letter. As the franks and newspapers accounted for a large part of the total mail, it was obvious that the abolition of the privilege for these two types of mailing piece of going free would materially reduce this average figure.

Next he showed the actual cost of carrying a letter from London to Edinburgh at the current rate of $1s$. $1d$. He estimated the total weight of the load on the coach—passengers, parcels, luggage, and so on—and accounted for every overhead cost incurred by coachmen, stage hands, and horses on the journey. The cost worked out at $\frac{1}{36}d$.! Three facts emerged from this: the first was that the rate was exorbitant; the second was that the difference in weight between one sheet of paper and several had such an infinitesimal effect on the carrying cost that greater tolerance about the number of sheets in each letter would be justified. Thirdly, the charge for carrying a letter could be uniform, because the actual mileage cost was a tiny proportion of the overall expenditure in conveying the letter from one address to another.

The difference between the $\frac{1}{36}d$. on the route from London to

Scotland and the $1\frac{1}{3}d$. cost on the average letter (which travelled a far shorter distance than the mileage of the Scottish route) indicated that collection and distribution overheads were inordinately heavy. The reason, as Rowland Hill pointed out, was that in the Post Offices large numbers of clerks were employed to check whether a letter was franked; if it was not, they had to weigh it, peer at it to see if there was more than one sheet, look up the mileage to the destination, and write down the charge. Where letters were delivered, the postmen had to knock at the door, wait for a reply, and collect the charges due; elsewhere, clerks had to be on duty at the Post Offices to receive the payments. If, suggested Rowland Hill, postage was prepaid at a uniform rate, all this tedious and intricate work would be abolished. '' It would soon be unnecessary to await the opening of the door, as every house might be provided with a letter-box into which the letter-carrier could drop the letter, and having knocked, he would pass on as fast as he could walk.''

Those with no head for figures and little interest in the economics of the Posts can be grateful to Rowland Hill for that sentence, because it brought that cheerful feature of our daily life which never fails to stir us, the morning rat-tat-tat which is the mark of the postman's arrival to-day.

Next came the concrete proposals of Rowland Hill's pamphlet. This was a penny-minded age. There were schools with a fee of $1d.$ a day. There was a journal called the *Penny Magazine* which was flooding the country. And in many towns there was the Penny Post. Rowland Hill felt confident that a general Penny Post would pay.

In his first pamphlet, Rowland Hill wanted the payment for letters to be made over the counter. The letter would then be postmarked with date and address of the office, indicating that $1d.$ had been taken. In the second edition of the pamphlet published a month later came another great idea which was destined to bring Rowland Hill world-wide fame. He solved problems of pre-payment by suggesting that the Post Office supply the sheets of paper for letters stamped with the information that $1d.$ had been paid. Envelopes were not, of course, in use at this time, and a letter was either folded so that the address could appear on the back or else it was enclosed in a simple wrapper. The idea of providing these stamped covers had already been suggested for newspapers, which did not go through the reception offices, but direct to the Post Office, and it was obvious that letters in such wrappers could be similarly handled even if the reception offices were closed.

There was, however, one obstacle. Business firms and private people alike employed messengers to take their correspondence to the Posts. Some were children; some the aged and infirm, who were glad of the small sums they could earn in this way. Such people often could not write. If they had letters written on plain paper they would not be able to address the stamped cover they then bought for 1d. A solution was offered by Hill in these charmingly written terms: " Perhaps this difficulty might be obviated by using a bit of paper just large enough to bear the stamp, and covered at the back with glutinous wash, which the bringer might, by applying a little moisture, attach to the back of the letter, so as to avoid the necessity of redirecting it."

The adhesive postage stamp had been invented.

The publication of Rowland Hill's views created polite interest among the authorities. A commission then sitting invited Hill to give his views on the London postal services—and as a result another publication was ready to languish on some dusty shelf, unnoticed and soon completely forgotten.

But the public interest in Rowland Hill's Penny Post was rising. The great reformers of the period were enthusiastic. Powerful business interests, bankers, lawyers, and industrialists started reading the pamphlet and praising it. In Parliament the persistent Robert Wallace demanded a select committee to examine Hill's proposals. In the House of Lords the Postmaster-General, the Earl of Lichfield, was provoked to exclaim testily " of all the wild and visionary schemes I have ever heard or read of, it is the most extraordinary ".

Then the young Victoria ascended the throne and a new Whig Government came into power. Robert Wallace got his Select Committee, and shortly afterwards a third edition of the pamphlet was published. This time the gentleness had gone. A preface lashed the lethargy of the Post Office, and the edition was enormously popular. Petitions began to arrive in at the House of Commons, some of the biggest coming from Scotland. A powerful body of London bankers and merchants had the ingenious idea of printing a newspaper, paying the 1*d*. stamp duty on it, and then posting it through the mails free. There resulted the quixotic situation that the Posts themselves helped willy-nilly in the campaign for their own reform. Members of Parliament were bombarded with all sorts of queer letters to show up the anomalies of the regulations. A tiny letter hardly to be read with the naked eye came through with double postage because it consisted of two sheets. Another, as large as a table cloth, arrived at single letter rates because it was only one sheet. Dickens' novels, then coming out in serial instalments, had advertisements about the Penny Post stitched into the centre pages of the story; cartoons of Queen Victoria questioning the Postmaster-General were distributed by the tens of thousands, and window bills calling on local folk to arrange meetings and sign petitions were pasted up throughout the country. Even by modern standards, the propaganda campaign which swept across Britain in 1837 and 1838 was an outstanding event which would do credit to the ingenuity of the most resourceful twentieth-century advertising agency. The banking house of Baring Brothers was largely responsible for the financing of the scheme.

The Post Office, naturally, fought back. Wallace's committee was given various estimates of the number of paid letters carried, mostly coloured in the direction to indicate that a 1*d*. rate would spell ruin. The real value of this body's work is that it discovered that people simply would not pay high rates. The regard for the law about postal monopoly had fallen so low that witness after witness frankly explained his particular method of evading postal charges. A publisher proudly announced that franks took care of his 6,000 or 7,000 business letters every year. Factory-owners stated that crates of goods from the works in the North were crammed with letters. Stage coaches carried them disguised as parcels. Booksellers, with their distribution organisation reaching every large town, had what amounted to a rival national system of Posts in their boxes. Baskets of food and sacks of vegetables from farms had their quota of mail tucked inside. Merchants had codes for letters (to be refused by the recipients) which gave market quotations in the addresses. The information of this kind in the Wallace Committee's report far outweighed the ominous forebodings of Lord Lichfield, who said that the volume of letters would have to be multiplied eight times in order to pay its way at a 1d. rate, and the Secretary's opinion that there would be a loss for forty or fifty years.

The general campaign grew bigger than ever. In 1839 no fewer than 2,000 petitions were presented in the House of Commons. One from the Lord Mayor and the citizens of the City of London carried 12,500 signatures which had been collected in a single day. Finally and inevitably, the historic day came. In July, 1839, the Chancellor of the Exchequer proposed to the House that the postage charged on letters should be reduced to a uniform rate of 1d. Peel, heading the Tories, objected because of the inevitable loss to the revenue at first, but the resolution went through with a twenty-to-one majority. Within a fortnight it had its Second Reading and went to the House of Lords. Grudgingly, the opponents there, represented by the Earl of Lichfield and the Duke of Wellington, agreed not to oppose the Bill (the Iron Duke said he voted for it " with great reluctance and pain "), and the Penny Post proposals became law on 17 August 1839.

By the end of the year the heavy black type of the Post Office announcement appeared all over the country:

Post Office Regulations

On and after the 10th January a letter not exceeding half an ounce in weight, may be sent from any part of the United Kingdom, to any other part, for One Penny, if paid when posted, or for Twopence if paid when delivered.

It was a mighty victory for the man from Kidderminster. To-day his statue stands outside the General Post Office, and some of the tokens of gratitude from the towns of Britain stand behind a case inside the public section of the G.P.O. itself.

9

LETTERS FOR EVERYBODY

IT is of interest to trace the growth of the letter-writing habit once the facility of cheap postage had been given to the people. As might be expected, it was neither the instant success Roland Hill and his friends had suggested, nor was it the ruinous experiment prophesied by its opponents. The organisation which saw the Penny Post through its birth throes was an unusual one. Rowland Hill was at the helm, but not as an official of the Post Office; he came under the Treasury. Both the Earl of Lichfield, his bitter opponent, and Colonel Maberley remained at the Post Office as Postmaster-General and Secretary.

The number of letters sent every week nearly doubled within a month of the Penny Post's inauguration, but the revenue decreased. Rowland Hill knew that it could drop quite a lot without undue alarm. When Queen Victoria came to the throne the average postal charge paid on a letter was $8\frac{3}{4}d.$, and out of the gross revenue of £2,340,000 the clear profit amounted to £1,650,000. The estimates arrived at by the Post Office accountants and Rowland Hill of the reduction in profit for the first year of operation had been £300,000. Actually—and Rowland Hill had clearly been too optimistic about the possibility of quickly changing a nation's letter-writing habits from the average of three a year that pertained during his campaign—the revenue drop in 1840 was more than £1,000,000. The extra letters handled had put up the expenditure by £100,000. However, there was still a healthy profit of £500,000 on the year's activities.

It may well be imagined how much criticism there was from those who had been overruled when Rowland Hill's miscalculations were known, and the fact that the Post Office finances were still perfectly sound, with evidence every week that the volume of letters was growing, seems to have been overlooked. Rowland Hill admitted frankly that he had been over-enthusiastic. He also rightly pointed out that the growing costs of the Posts, chiefly due to the high rates for railway carriage as compared with the mail coaches, could not have been visualised beforehand. Nor could Rowland Hill take direct action to put things right. In his position at the Treasury, he could only recommend to the Chancellor of the Exchequer that he should tell the Postmaster-General to do this or that.

In August 1841 the Treasury, in its position as the body responsible for approving expenditure on Post Office services, pointed out that the revenue did not justify the extension of a postal service to every part of the Kingdom. Before the advent of the Penny Posts there had been, as we have learned, the local Penny Posts and the Fifth Clause Posts, both of which were designed to carry the costs of local distribution without adding to the general overheads of the basic organisation. With Rowland Hill's scheme in operation, this extra revenue had, of course, disappeared.

A sensible compromise was devised. The number of post offices in every district were to be in proportion to the number of the population and the area in which they lived. This meant that, geographically, the offices would be closer in densely populated areas (such as the Black Country and the Lancashire textile towns), but more numerous, in relation to the number of persons per post office, in rural areas such as the Dales of Yorkshire or Central Wales.

It was a very fair arrangement and worked out so that there was in practice a post office in every registrar's district. This extension of the postal service did not yet provide delivery to the homes of every correspondent. Who should have a door-to-door delivery and who should not created some discussion between the Treasury and the Post Office, the arguments being settled by Peel who decided that by June 1843 the service should be based on the number of letters in each locality. In all districts where 100 letters were the weekly average of the incoming mail, the inhabitants were entitled to a receiving office and a daily delivery.

In the eighteen months that were occupied in setting up this organisation the new Posts numbered 692, and they handled an average of 200 letters a week each. They represented a far larger number of villages, for the majority of the receiving offices were placed centrally to cover two or more villages (the average worked out at three communities per Post). Good as it was as compared with the position five years before, it left a lot to be desired with many thousands of villages without delivery service of any kind. One reason for the slow development of the rural Posts was that the regulations provided for a daily service or none at all. In addition, some isolated communities were given a service simply because they could guarantee 100 letters a week, while others, quite close to towns, were ignored because they were too small to be able to reach the necessary figure. From a financial viewpoint, the former service might be running at a loss, while the latter would be near enough to pay its way with a mere score or so of letters, as it would merely require a foot Post to walk over with the mail.

In 1850 the principle was changed so that a Post was established so long as it could pay its way. This was taken to be the case if a letter could be delivered for $\frac{1}{2}d$. A modest volume always developed rapidly as soon as the service was started, thereby rapidly decreasing the cost per letter to a fraction of $\frac{1}{2}d$. Few districts were unable to meet these reasonable requirements, particularly as the $\frac{1}{2}d$. ruling would apply even if it could be reached only by restricting the posts to delivery once a week. A whole host of places quickly obtained a service by which the post-man called once, twice, or three times weekly.

Three years later there were further improvements. Postal deliveries were increased from one a day to a greater frequency if the letters justified a service on the cost basis of $\frac{1}{4}d$. each, and by 1856 the Postmaster-General was able to announce that 300,000 letters a week, apart from newspapers and books, were being delivered free. In 1863, the year before Sir Rowland Hill resigned, the ten-year campaign to increase the free delivery services had benefited 10,000 places, and more than 94 per cent. of all mailing pieces were handed direct to the recipient without extra charge. This still left 24 millions which had to be collected from a

JOHN PALMER

One of the sights of London in the early nineteenth century: mail coach starting time outside the General Post Office. The dome of St. Paul's can be seen. The famous Bull and Mouth inn (on which site part of the G.P.O. now stands) can be seen in

The pioneer mail coach running between London and Bath.

receiving office. The climax came when, as part of the celebrations of Queen Victoria's Diamond Jubilee, free delivery was guaranteed to every house in the country. More than 100,000 people were then working on behalf of the Royal Mail, a great proportion of them the postmen and the postwomen who plodded day in and day out, winter and summer alike, to the loneliest home of a Highland crofter or the stone cottage hidden on Dartmoor. Nearly 2,000 million letters were being carried in the postmen's satchels, and most of their journeys were made on foot, for in studying the comparatively slow growth of a truly national delivery service to everyone's front door, it must be realised that the invaluable device which made, and still makes, the postman's lot an easier one—the bicycle— did not arrive until the national arrangements had been put into force. The more difficult journeys were accomplished on horseback. In some hilly areas this relic of the same mode of travel as that of the earliest Posts in the fifteenth century still continues in present times. The last Welsh mounted postman, for example, died just before the 1939-45 War. He rode on a long and mountainous round in Caernarvonshire, and in his career covered more than a quarter of a million miles. Horses are still used on Dartmoor and in Yorkshire.

During the fifty-seven years that elapsed between the start of the Penny Post in 1840 and the inauguration of the national service as we know it to-day in 1897, the gross revenue of the Post Office indicates the enormous increase in letter writing which the provision of cheap and universal facilities engendered. In 1840 the figure was £1,359,466; in 1897-8 it was £12,420,376. (In 1949-50 the income from postal business was £83,944,025.)

The growth of letter-writing was a profound social revolution. It came at a time when people had need to write to one another as never before. The calls of the industrial machine were bringing armies of people from the villages into the towns. In the Midlands and Lancashire, as well as Yorkshire and the Scottish Lowlands, entire villages were literally left with only the old folk in them. Immigrants from Ireland arrived in their tens of thousands yearly. By 1841 the Irish population in Lancashire was estimated to have reached 133,000, and after the failure of the potato crop in the forties, another half a million arrived before 1851. The cost

4

of the passage from Liverpool dropped from 2s. 6d. at the turn of the century to 4d. or 5d. by 1830. Admittedly, many of these people were illiterate, but the majority of them could communicate with home in some fashion, even if the letter had to be written by a friend and read by the village priest in the native village. Some idea of the movement of English people into manufacturing towns can be obtained from a comparison of the population figures of 1831 and 1851 for typical areas. Manchester and Salford went up from 237,000 to 400,000; Leeds from 123,000 to 172,000; Bolton from 42,000 to 61,000; Halifax from 22,000 to 34,000; Sheffield from 93,000 to 135,000; and Bradford from 44,000 to 104,000. For these workpeople, living in squalor in the towns, often leaving home at twelve or thirteen, both for them and their relations who remained in the villages the advent of the Penny Post must have been a real gleam of happiness in the never-ending round of work, and the friends of Rowland Hill who suggested that his innovation had ensured the peacefulness of the working classes by giving them some anchor with family life did not exaggerate.

In addition to the Penny Post on letters, many other innovations were made after 1840 which, familiar as they are to-day, were then innovations which materially increased the correspondence habit. Among the most novel was the transmission of Christmas cards. The Christmas card became popular very slowly. The idea was thought of shortly after the introduction of the Penny Post. The honour is generally given to W. C. Dobson, a Royal Academician whose Biblical paintings were extremely popular with Queen Victoria. In 1844 he painted a card symbolical of Christmas and sent it to a friend instead of the formal letter of good wishes which had become customary at that period. For the Christmas of 1845, Dobson had the design lithographed and he posted it to a large number of friends.

Dobson does not seem to have realised the commercial possibilities of the Christmas card. Another man who had also thought of a picture as a good form of festive message must claim the title of the first commercial Christmas card artist. He was Sir Henry Cole, who had been appointed Rowland Hill's assistant in 1839. Cole was an amateur artist. He considered the possibilities as early as 1843, but it was not until the winter of 1846 that his design appeared in the stationers' shops. Although he made the sketches, the finished card was the work of J. C. Horsley, later an R.A. and painter of several of the frescoes in the Houses of Parliament.

The picture on this 1846 card was superimposed on a trellis-work round three panels. The centre panel showed a family group with the words "A Merry Christmas and a Good New Year to You "; the two side panels represented " feeding the poor " and " clothing the naked ". About 1,000 copies were lithographed and then painted by hand. To-day the original card has a collector's value of £50, though anyone who finds one in an old family album should not become too excited. There have been periodical reprints of the card which are of little monetary value.

By Christmastide 1847 other artists were producing Christmas cards. Perhaps the best known of the early examples is the design by the Rev. W. E. Bradley, a Newcastle clergyman, whose card was lithographed by a local printing firm and put on general sale in the North-east.

At first the cards had their enemies. The Cole-Horsley design was attacked by the powerful temperance organisations of the day because the family in the centre panel were happily quaffing wine. Not until the 'seventies did the Christmas card become anything but a bizarre novelty. In that decade Sir Adolph Tuck, son of the founder of the world-famous firm of fine art printers, took the Christmas card in hand. Well-known artists of the day were invited to submit designs. They were exhibited in London galleries in the summer alongside the work of unknowns, who entered the competitions in which large prizes were offered. With this publicity, the Christmas card idea caught on, and the Post Office began to experience an avalanche of them in the first weeks of December. German printers also saw the possibilities and began to flood the country with cheap cards printed from designs by Bavarian artists. As these men were instructed to produce a Christmassy scene, they illustrated the cards with the deep snow which they knew in their country, and from this, incidentally, has grown the legend that an "old-fashioned English Christmas" invariably included drifts of snow almost to the eaves of the house. It was no truer then than it is now.

The postcard was another facility which enormously increased the number of mailing pieces handled by the Post Office. Austria was the first country to use them. Exactly a year after their introduction in that country, on 1 October 1870, the British Post Office put them on sale. No charge was made for them, and they could be posted for $\frac{1}{2}d$. The postcard was an obvious bargain and, to the annoyance of the stationers, enormous numbers were sold. In a little more than a year they were passing through the mails at the rate of nearly $1\frac{1}{2}$ millions a week. In the following year a charge of $\frac{1}{2}d$. per dozen was made for postcards, apart from the $\frac{1}{2}d$. postage, and private cards were allowed to pass impressed with a stamp by the Inland Revenue Department. The imposition of a charge for the card, even though it was nominal and mainly to offset the complaints of the stationers about unfair competition by the Crown, caused a slight drop in popularity, but by 1874 they were exceeding the $1\frac{1}{2}$ millions a week total of 1871.

In 1894, a card with an adhesive stamp passed as a postcard, and as part of the Diamond Jubilee concessions the prohibition of writing or printing on the address side was removed. This small concession engendered a craze which no one could possibly have envisaged. Within ten years the number of postcards sent through the mails leapt to an average of 16 millions a week. The postcard craze died in the way that crazes will. Even the most enthusiastic sender of postcards from his holiday resort cannot imagine the extent of the postcard business at the turn of the century. Almost every home had an album in which all postcards received were kept. The crudely comic card which sails dangerously near contravening the regulations as regards the despatch through the mails of indecent or obscene prints or paintings, was one popular type to send to one's friends; but far bigger sales were achieved by the conventional view postcard and the story card. The latter, often by a well-known artist, illustrated some dramatic episode concerning the Boer War, or merely an incident of romantic life given a thoughtful title such as " The Parting " or " The Meeting ". Some of these cards were rather like a serial in which the enthusiastic recipient, providing his correspondent kept mailing the next instalment, could read a complete life-story, full of drama, tragedy, and surprise in every picture.

The barrack-rooms of the troops of the last war, with their rows of glossy pin-ups printed in Hollywood, had their counterpart in the troopships and tents of the men who fought in the Boer War. Postcards which showed the most popular actresses and music-hall stars of the day had enormous sales. They were certainly not of the " leg style " we know to-day, for even an artist whose dialogue and songs caused strong men to blench and the womenfolk hurriedly to leave the theatre were shown as ethereal beauties surrounded by flowers and even a Cupid or two. The picture post-card age has never died. Most people send a few while they are on holiday to friends and relations, whereas they certainly would not trouble to write a letter. The innovation started for the benefit of the impecunious; it has remained as an economical and simple method of sending brief messages. On either basis it has been one of the most popular innovations of the past 100 years by the Post Office. In 1948-9 the inland mails carried 216 million cards—only a quarter of the peak total of yesteryear, but still a formidable source of revenue.

No account of the spread of the mail services would be complete without some details of the newspaper post. News sheets rapidly increased under Cromwell, and most of them depended for circulation on a national scale on transmission through the Posts. At least this was the case where the regularity of the official services was more attractive than any of the " contraband " arrangements for carrying mail existing at that time. The time-lag on delivery in distant parts of the country was steady, and despatch could be arranged for a set time every day—an invaluable advantage for the publishers. The early journals of this time bore titles which clearly show their close relationship with the Posts. The *Protestant Postboy*, the *Flying Post*, and the *Post* are typical. Very often these journals included a blank section where the subscriber could write a letter to his friend. A newspaper tax was first imposed in 1711 at a rate of $\frac{1}{2}d$. per copy. This tax was periodically increased until by the year of the French Revolution it had reached 2*d*. Partly because the very first news-sheet had been semi-official (the *London Gazette*, first issued in the year of the Plague, 1665) and partly as a tacit return for payment of tax, newspapers had always gone through the Posts free of charge.

Many, indeed, had been started as news bulletins by the P.O. surveyors who found them a profitable sideline.

Any perquisites from the sale of newspapers sent by mail belonged by tradition to the Clerks of the Road; these were the men appointed to organise the service along a particular route, and their office dated back to Charles II. They had started with a weekly wage of 25*s.* a week, and even 100 years later their salary was quite nominal, though the privilege of franking all newspapers for free transit brought them £8,000 a year. As there were only six clerks at the time, the job was certainly a desirable one, though they had considerable expenses to pay to their assistants, whom they employed on their own behalf. In 1764 the privilege of franking newspapers was granted to Members of Parliament, ostensibly so that they could have copies sent to their homes when the Commons were not sitting, but in practice to any address if they signed their names outside. There resulted the practice of members making an agreement with a bookseller or publisher to sign all the newspaper wrappers desired—and no doubt eulogistic comments about the politician concerned appeared in the editorials as a *quid pro quo*. It therefore resulted that, either through the Clerk of the Roads, an M.P. or official of the Government, every newspaper went free. The Chancellor of the Exchequer probably turned a blind eye to the practice, for the more papers that were sold the more tax he received. The law that was passed in 1825, allowing newspapers to pass free, was really a formality to regularise a system which had existed for years.

The resourceful Palmer, inventor of the mail coach, opened a Newspaper Office in 1787 which dealt only with the newspaper Posts. Although he found himself in trouble because he started the office without a by-your-leave from anyone, it was a great benefit to the Clerks of the Letter Office, who loathed the flood of wet and heavy newspapers which arrived at the last minute and had to be frantically sorted in order to catch the mail coaches.

The tax rose to 4*d.* by the end of the Napoleonic Wars (which meant *The Times*, for example, then cost 7*d.*), but by this time the newspaper-reading habit was so thoroughly instilled in the public's mind, largely due to anxiety for news of the progress of

hostilities, that even this heavy burden, called "a tax on knowledge" by its critics, did not seemingly reduce the circulation.
By the time of the eventual reduction of the tax to 1*d*., 45,000
newspapers were sent to the Newspaper Office every night, and
200 clerks dealt with them.

When the newspaper stamp duty was abolished in 1855, the
daily papers, as well as publications appearing less frequently,
were still permitted to go free if they bore an impressed stamp.
In other words, a publisher could decide to continue paying the
tax if he wished; in return, he had free postage. Obviously, the
choice depended on the size of his provincial readership and postal
subscribers. If it were a major proportion of his circulation, it
paid him to continue. If, on the other hand, he had a local
circulation within the boundaries of a town, then he could well
afford to dispense with the franking privilege.

Actually the reduction in the number of newspapers going
through the post free was large, immediately falling by 25 per cent.
a year by 1864, and in 1870 free newspaper transit was finally
abolished. The new arrangement was that a newspaper, no matter
how heavy, could go for ½*d*., the publication consisting of "wholly
or in great part of political or other news, or of articles relating
thereto, or to other current topics"; it had to be printed and
published in Great Britain, and appear at intervals of not more
than seven days. At the present time, of course, a publication
has to be registered with the G.P.O. as meeting the provisions as
regards news and frequency of appearance, and the inland rate of
1½*d*. for 4 oz., plus ½*d*. for each additional 4 oz. per copy, is still
the cheapest form of postal service there is.

Although the Post Office was strangely dilatory in the setting up
of a parcel Post, what was to all intents and purposes a special
organisation began in 1848, when Rowland Hill managed to overcome the opposition of the railways and start a book post.

The Government, as well as many social workers and leaders
of the Church, were genuinely anxious to enhance the moral and
social standards of the people by education for both children and
adults. Many ambitious and ingenious schemes were started to
release the people from ignorance, and the very foundation of all
these schemes was obviously to teach them to read, and, after

they had been so taught, to encourage them to write. The situation was alarming by any standard. Since 1839 the Registrar-General had been keeping figures of the number of people who signed their marriage certificates with a mark. It remained roughly the same at the disgraceful figure of 40 per cent. of the total for nine years.

Sunday schools, workers' institutes, and evening classes were started to remedy this state of affairs, and the publishing industry energetically strove to supply the books and magazines which were needed to maintain the people's interest. Books could be sent through the post at the rate of 6d. per pound, and in 1855 the rates were reduced to 4 oz. for 1d., 8 oz. for 2d., and 1 lb. for 4d. At the new rates about 3 million books were despatched during the year, a large proportion of them from lending libraries. It was a great and generous service in the cause of education conducted by the Post Office—one for which it deserves the highest commendation, for it cannot have been a very profitable venture until the printed-matter rates came into operation in 1870, when the total of books, circulars, catalogues, and so on rose in twelve months from 130 million to 202 million (these figures including newspapers).

It will have been noted that in these services of the Post Office the peak of development came in the mid-nineteenth century. Behind them stands Sir Rowland Hill.

For his post at the Treasury he had been offered £500, later raised to £1,500 because of protests. Not a small part of his daily routine was the waging of a prolonged and bitter war with Colonel Maberley. His recommendation that the Post Office Secretary should be transferred to some other department was turned down, and by 1842 Rowland Hill himself, maybe because governments never favoured trouble-makers, was told that his services were no longer needed. His dismissal was undoubtedly mixed up with politics, and the change of Government thus was the reason quite as much as any intriguing by the heads of the Post Office. Not unnaturally, the public at large thought their hero had been served a very scurvy trick. Petitions were organised and protest meetings held. Powerful business interests organised a testimonial which reached £13,000. After he had spent four years in the political wilderness, a Whig Government came to power and a new post was created for Rowland Hill—that of Secretary to the Postmaster-General. Colonel Maberley remained as Secretary to the Post Office. This uneasy partnership continued until 1854, when Maberley resigned and Rowland Hill was given his job.

The personal troubles which persisted to the bitter end between the two men were not entirely Colonel Maberley's fault. Rowland Hill appears to have had the single-mindedness of a man with a mission, which, however valuable in order to get things done, tends to create a sense of intolerance and impatience with all obstacles and criticism. Anthony Trollope, who wrote many of his novels in the spare time which a postal official such as he was seems to have had, disliked Rowland Hill. He wrote that the man was at home with facts and figures, but had little understanding of men. Certainly even the rank and file of the Post Office learned to dislike him, once Rowland Hill was in the position of Secretary. They were overworked and underpaid.

Rowland Hill had begun his campaign for the Penny Post at the age of thirty-eight. When he really came into control in 1854, he was sixty. Until he was seventy he ran the Post Office with the vigour of a man half his age. Scores of the changes he made were concerned with the internal organisation, which, though possibly of little public interest, indicate how modern were his views. Others were obvious to all. Pillar boxes went up in lavish quantities; London was divided into districts (without the numbers we know to-day); the quarterly *Post Office Guide* and the first of the *Annual Reports* (without which a volume such as this would have been impossible) were started in 1855.

On the whole Rowland Hill got on quite well with the Postmasters-General of his decade in the office of Secretary. The exception was Lord Stanley, appointed in 1860. There does not seem to have been any definite reason for the quarrel, though Lord Stanley was certainly not content to regard his job as a sinecure, as had been the practice by some of his predecessors. Whatever the reason, two strong-willed men clashed continually. The result was inevitable. Rowland Hill resigned in 1864, after six months' leave of absence through ill health. There was naturally some talk in Parliament and the Press that the long-drawn-out war between

the Post Office hierarchy and its reformer had resulted in the
defeat of the latter. At least this was not ostensibly so. His
Queen, his erstwhile enemies, both Houses of Parliament, and
scores of public bodies went out of their way to give him the
acknowledgments of a job well done that was his due. His salary
was changed into a life pension, and Parliament voted him a
grant of £20,000. Honorary degrees came to add lustre to his
knighthood. Probably of greater reward than any of these things
was the size of the Post he had worked for twenty-four years to
develop. Every minute of the year 2,500 letters were dropped into
the Post Office boxes, bearing the stamps he had thought of and
carried at the rates he had advocated—a mighty torrent of 675
million a year at the time of his retirement. To-day more than
8,000 million items are posted every year, 160 for every man,
woman, and child in the country. At the time of Sir Rowland
Hill's birth, the average was three.

Sir Rowland Hill lived to spend fifteen years in retirement. He
was buried with other great figures of British history, among the
warriors, the politicians, and the poets, in Westminster Abbey.
His real memorial travels by air, sea, and land to the four corners
of the earth: a little coloured piece of paper bearing the portrait
of the King and the words " Postage Revenue ".

10

ROYAL MAIL BY SEA

As we have seen, up to the end of the reign of Elizabeth, such mail services by boat as were run by the Government were chiefly for the benefit of court officials, and would apply roughly to the diplomatic bags and the courier services of the King's Messengers of to-day. Merchants and foreigners who wished to write to people in Europe made their own arrangements. It was not until 1619 that an effort was made to place the foreign Posts in official hands. In that year a Patent of James I established a Postmaster for Foreign Parts out of the King's Domains, with Mathew de Quester and his son being appointed to run the office. They did very little to improve matters, and it was not until Thomas Witherings succeeded them in March 1633 that a through service to the Continent was organised. It seems that the cross-Channel service—the packet-boats—were merely row-boats.

In contrast to the Continental route, the mail service to Ireland had been regularly running for years. It has already been explained how special vessels were hired for the sea passage to Ireland as early as 1598, when Sir John Stanhope organised a shuttle service between Holyhead and Dublin, paying £20 a month to the owners for their services. Now, thirty-five years later, Witherings organised a somewhat similar service across the Straits of Dover. The Dover boatmen were engaged to take the mail immediately on arrival in the port and to carry nothing else, remaining in Calais until the reply was ready.

In the ensuing years the chief concern of the Post Office was to see that the monopoly of the internal Posts was maintained once letters were delivered to an English seaport. No one much cared about the means by which they arrived. The first enactment concerning ships' letters was passed in 1657, and this was made more specific by another Act in 1660. This legislation provided that homecoming vessels were to give up all letters on arrival in port. Such was the law, but ships' masters evidently ignored it, for soon afterwards we find in the Post Office accounts details of payments made at the rate of 1d. for every letter handed over. In 1692 the Treasury questioned the Post Office about the legality of these payments, and the reply stated that, while there was no authority for them, the provisions of the law were insufficient to compel its observance and the 1d. allowance had become a customary inducement at all the principal ports.

The 1660 Act was one of the many pieces of legislation passed during the gradual return to normal conditions after the Restoration. The English cross-Channel service was sailing from Dover twice a week. In addition, there was French service sailing from Calais. The incoming mail was thus carried by French boats under a financial arrangement with the French Post Office, and this happy augury of future international liaison on matters of foreign Posts was unfortunately brought to nought when war between the two countries broke out in 1689. But the close ties with the Netherlands which had been created by Charles II while in exile had resulted before this time in another packet-boat route being opened, between Harwich and Helvoetsluis in Holland. Three sturdy sloops maintained this service.

More packet-boat services were also started to Ireland. In addition to the Holyhead and Dublin service, there was the Southern Ireland route between Milford Haven and Waterford, and a third which made use of the short sea passage between Port Patrick, Scotland, and Donaghadee, near Belfast.

Still more important was the inauguration of the foreign Post ships specially for mercantile interests between Falmouth and Corunna in Spain. It proved extremely successful and was extended to our oldest ally, Portugal, with a Falmouth-Lisbon service. Here it was possible for letters to connect with the many vessels sailing to the New World. The packet boats on these routes were armed, for they were constantly in danger from French privateers, and they had to sail well to the west of Cherbourg and

Brest to avoid attack in the periodic wars with France which marked the turn of the seventeenth century.

Even though the foreign postal service was becoming so wide-spread, the number of letters was still small, and the special section set up in London known as the Foreign Post Office employed only a score or so of men all told. The real trouble was that merchants and shippers had to send bills of lading and check notes with their goods, and they naturally included business correspondence with them sooner than pay for ordinary mail services which, in any event, would not necessarily arrive at the same time as the goods to which the letters obviously in part referred. Despite the growing financial burden, in 1702 a regular service with the West Indies and the English colonies in America was started. The ships were to run with a maximum of 5 tons of goods and a few passengers and attempt to sail to a schedule. It was maintained, despite the attacks of the French and the storms of Atlantic winters, for nine years, in which period a dozen ships were lost from various causes. In terms of men and vessels, the loss was terrible, and in the more mundane considerations of balancing the revenue from the foreign mails with the costs of running the vessels on their six months' round trip it was clearly an unrealistic proposition.

After that experiment, the packet boat connections to the New World were by temporarily hired vessels. Sometimes, for urgent official letters, they sailed with mail and passengers only. More usually the normal merchant route would be followed.

On the short sea services from Harwich, Dover, Holyhead, and so on, the ships were about 70 tons and on the ocean routes from Falmouth the tonnage ranged from 150 and 170. The Commissioners of Fees and Gratuities who enquired into the conduct of the packet service in 1788 expressed the view that the " burthen of the Falmouth Packets should be 150 tons and their complement of eighteen men ".

Working as intermediaries between the Postmasters-General and the commanders of the packets were agents, whose duty it was to see that the conditions of the contracts were duly fulfilled, especially as regards the equipment of the ships, the complement of the crews, and the payment of wages. The contracts were for seven, fourteen, or twenty-one years, and as, once a packet was hired, the Post Office paid all wear and tear and miscellaneous expenses and, in case of capture by an enemy, paid also to the owner the original cost of the vessel, the packet establishment became very costly.

The agents were given much power; and it is clear from the official records that their power was grossly abused, especially at Falmouth, the Commissioners of Enquiry already alluded to reporting in the year 1788 that the management of the packets had become " an unbounded source of Expense and Peculation ". The scandal must have lasted many years; for in 1777 it is recorded in a letter from Lord George Germain to William Knox, Under-Secretary for the Colonial Department, that the King had spoken about the bad state of the packet boats, and had ordered representations on the subject to be made to the Post Office. Unfortunately, the Post Office itself was deeply implicated. Although, as already stated, the packets were hired from their commanders, the Commission of Enquiry found that in many cases officials of the Post Office were the actual owners of the packets, and that the principal officer in this department (the Secretary) received in one way and another emoluments from the Packet Service which in the course of seventeen years amounted to little less than £50,000. Needless to say, there was a tremendous scandal at the time. The result was that no official of the Post Office was thereafter allowed to have any direct or indirect interest in the packets.

These were troublesome times. First there was the war with the colonists of America, and then the long period of hostilities with France after the French Revolution. The fact that the packets contained both letters of vital importance for the country's strategy overseas and also bullion for the financing of her own forces and for her allies made the vessels a delectable target both for the enemy navies and to freebooters merely after riches. The packets were well armed, so that they could defend themselves—so well, in fact, that there are some strange stories about packet-boat commanders who not only fought back hard when attacked, but also went out spoiling for a fight. These men did, in short, go in for a little amateur piracy while on their lawful journeyings. It was to take away this temptation that a Committee of Enquiry suggested that the packets should be unarmed and rely on speed for safety. The Post Office protested about this, and there was a compromise in a sort of armament limitation, the cannon and the small arms provided being quite useless for offensive action, but a slight means of last-stand defence. The instructions ordered the mail to be brought on deck and weighted with chains as soon as an enemy sail was sighted. A sailor stood ready to jettison the bags if boarding seemed imminent.

It was a harsh order which, one would suggest, only a committee sitting safely in London would have put forward. The hopeless odds in any engagement with a well-armed enemy ship demanded heroism which, however noble, entailed needless sacrifice of English lives, and it is amazing that the orders seemed to have been obeyed without protest by the seamen. The gallantry of the men who sailed the packets is typified in the letters sent to the Treasury about an engagement between the *Atlanta*, a French privateer, and the *Antelope*, a Falmouth packet-boat bound for Jamaica.

The first was written by the Lieutenant-Governor of Jamaica:

There were but 14 men capable of doing duty when they were attacked by the Privateer, all the rest were ill with fevers. Their victory was entirely owing to the Passengers, as the Officers were killed early in the Action. Great praise is given to Mr. Nodin, a Passenger, who was formerly a Midshipman, and from his knowledge of working the ship stood by the helm armed with a Pike and Musquet, which he alternatively made use of as he found occasion. Colonel Loppinott's account of him surpasses all description. When he saw the Men climbing up the sides he immediately quitted the helm, seized his lance and sent them to oblivion, then returned to his helm, Righted the ship and seized his Musquet, loaded and flew to Quarters, and being a good Marksman was sure of dropping a Man every time he fired. In this great exertion was Mr. Nodin for an Hour and a quarter. They being locked alongside Mr. Nodin had an opportunity of taking good aim. Then success also depended on the conduct of the Boatswain, for when the Privateer grappled he lashed the Schooner forward fast to the Ship so that when the Rascals were swept off the deck, and when they wished to get away they could not, nor could a Man go forward to cast off but he was immediately shot by Mr. Nodin, and the ship being so much higher than the Privateer, gave the Packet People great advantage. Mr. Nodin in one of their attempts to board killed four or five Men. The Privateer had 65 men besides six or eight Blacks. Twenty odd lay dead on the deck when they called for quarters, besides several that must have dropped into the Sea. About 30 Men including wounded were landed. Great Praise is also due to Colonel Loppinott, his poor Secretary who fell dead, and Mr. Bryant's Servant, Monsieur Cazeau. Colonel Lopinott, who knew the Captain of the Privateer, says he was a very great Rascal; on Board the Privateer there were a vast quantity of cloaths, both of Ladies and Gentlemen, and which it is supposed they had pilfered from on Board different Vessels which have fallen into their clutches.

The second is:

An exact account of the *Antelope's* Action with the *Atlanta*, prepared by the crew.

December 1st. At 8 a.m., being off Cumberland Harbour five leagues, We saw two schooners which gave chase. We kept Ship to the S. to avoid them, but soon found one of them coming up fast, but outsailed the other.

December 2nd. At 4 p.m., Chace about Gunshot from us. Hoisted our Colours; she hoisted French Colours and the Bloody Flag, and gave us her Bow Chaces, which we returned with our Stern Chaces. All night running with the Schooner in Sight, which kept us at our Quarters all night. At 5 a.m. she sheared up and gave us a Broadside, which We returned; she then clapped us alongside and grappled us in a very hot Fire. At the same time observed them dividing themselves to board us on the Bow and Quarter; the 15 Men that were appointed to board us forward were killed by the Shot and Grape from the two foremost Guns, but there being no Guns aft, they got up, but were deceived by our Boarding Netting

A mail coach picking up and dropping mail without stopping — forerunner of the railway travelling Post Office. Picture painted about 1838.

The Lion Hotel, Shrewsbury. Its eighteenth century landlord, Robert Lawrence, was responsible for diverting the London-Holy-

This 15th century inn at Colchester became one of the great coaching and posting houses of the Eastern counties. Twenty coaches a day clattered through the archway below the lamp.

The Angel and Royal at Grantham was familiar to every mail carrier from the days of the Tudor Posts to the 19th century

and Handspikes. Captain Curtis in that Sally with a Passenger and the Steward got killed, and Mr. Mitchell badly wounded. We then kept up a constant Fire with Round, Grape and Musquetry, and she then made another attempt to Board us by cutting down the Boarding Nettings, Ridge Ropes, &c., but they all got killed in the attempt. Our loss this Sally was 3 more wounded. They then tried to get off by cutting their Grappling Rope, but were prevented by the Boatswain locking her square Sail Yard to our Fore Shrouds. We directly after found her Fire slacken, which greatly encouraged us. We kept up a constant fire for half an Hour more, when We had the Pleasure of hearing them cry for Mercy. But by all appearance they deserved none, nor expected any, as some of them jumped overboard and drowned themselves, for their bloody Flag was nailed to the Masthead. They were then ordered to tear it down, and We then took Possession, which it was lucky it was so soon, for our Main Sail, Netting, Quarter Cloths and Hammocks were on Fire, which in the midst of the Fire and Smoke was not seen. To save the Ship was obliged to cut all away.

Antelope sailed with 29 men in all from Falmouth:

4 Men dead before the Action, 2 very Sick at the time, which left 23 including the Doctor.

3 Killed, 4 wounded. A French Gentleman, Passenger, killed, who with another French Gentleman, was all that assisted the Ship's Company.

Privateer had 8 carriage Guns and—

65 Men.

50 Killed, wounded, and Missing;

15 Men unhurt.

Witness to their signing Wm. Curgenven.	}	The Marks of	{	O. Jno. Pasco, Boatswain. X. Peter Bundle, Gunner.

The contents of the cargoes which went on the transatlantic

5

packets were varied indeed. Agents' letter-books include such bizarre items as:

Fifteen couple of hounds.

Some parcels of cloth for the Clothing Colonels in my Lord North's and my Lord Grey's regiments.

Two servant maids going as laundresses to my Lord ambassador Methuen.

By 1798 the troubles of a mounting pile of overseas mail and of getting it through the world at war resulted in the establishment of a Ship Letter Office. This was an attempt to regularise the despatch of mails by ordinary merchant vessels. The idea was to adapt what was already happening in any event and to maintain in fact as well as in law the monopoly. In every coffee-house in London, which were the places where such present-day institutions as Lloyd's and the Stock Exchange had their origins, bags were hung up on posts for the collection of merchants' letters for destinations overseas. They were labelled with the name of the ship, the date of sailing, and the ports of call. The system of payment for this service is not known, but the coffee-house Post undoubtedly gave a cheaper service and probably a more reliable one. The Post Office realised that, if it prohibited this system, it could not offer anything to replace it, so it simply proposed that the bags of letters should be collected by the Post Office, be stamped and charged, sent by mail coach to the port from which the ship was sailing, and handed over to the master of the ship for transport overseas. The rates by this service were to be half those for the normal packets, and the ship's master got 2d. for every letter he took. The Ship Letter Office started work on 10 September 1799 and gained some slight popularity, for at least it ensured that the captain handled the mail with care instead of failing to deliver it, as sometimes happened. Nevertheless, an enormous amount of "contraband mail" still continued under the old method. Some merchants made no charge for this little service to their business friends when they actually owned the ships used, and others required nothing beyond a gratuity for their captains. Not until the currency export restrictions of the present time have there been such energetic efforts by the Customs and

Excise to prevent unauthorised mail leaving the country. The zealous efficiency of the Customs officers in seizing mail bags on ships about to leave port proved something of an embarrassment to the Post Office. When the letters were handed over to them, they became mail which had to be dealt with. As the correspondence was not paid for, the letters had to be opened, the senders asked for payment of the correct amount, and the letters re-sealed and sent on their way. The merchants violently protested at all this red tape and delay, and the Treasury warned the Post Office that it was on tricky legal ground in pursuing its policy.

In 1818 the enraged officials, noting that bags still hung openly in the coffee-houses, made a test prosecution of the proprietor of the New England Coffee-house for the illegal collection of letters. The action was withdrawn on the payment of £5 and the publication of apology in the newspapers. It was a tacit admission by the Post Office of defeat, and by 1827 the coffee-house mail bags were more numerous and fuller than ever. Not until all previous Post Office Acts were repealed and the new Act passed in 1837 was the contraband Post finally vanquished.

Before this the official packet services had been improving, which was the best method of ensuring that all letters went that way. The reason was the coming of steam and the consequent lessening of delays through contrary winds and bad weather. Even in 1816 a steamer was plying between England and Ireland; she was the *Hibernia*, a vessel of 112 tons, and she was the first ship to use steam on any cross-Channel route from the United Kingdom. It does not seem to have ever helped with the mails, but five years later the *Lightning*, a larger ship of 205 tons, regularly carried the mail between Holyhead and Dublin. Its success resulted in the establishment of steam packet services by Government-owned vessels to Calais, Ostend, Portugal, and the Mediterranean.

The building of expensive steam-driven vessels for the trans-ocean routes was obviously uneconomic, and the Post Office approached the owners of the merchant steamers for help in carrying mails.

The steamship *Sirius* left England for America on 31 March 1838, and carried a ship mail consisting of over 300 letters and

50 newspapers. As soon as it was learned that she and another steamship, the *Great Western*, could perform the voyage in safety, the public was quick to take advantage of the new and speedy channel for the despatch of correspondence to their friends in the New World; and the mails rapidly increased in bulk. The Government was as eager as the public to benefit by the new order of things, and proposed to despatch by the *Great Western*, instead of by its own sailing packets, the public despatches and ordinary letter bags, and to pay for the service the gratuities authorised for ships' masters.

The running costs of these large steam-driven ships on the Atlantic route bore no comparison with those for a small sailing vessel, and the owners of the *Great Western* simply refused the Post Office order that they were to carry mails in return for this gratuity. They called it a pittance, and said that the mail could go in the *Great Western* if half the postage on every letter was handed over. This the Post Office considered unreasonable and offered a flat rate of £200 for the round trip from England to America. This tender was also rejected. It seems that once again the legal aspects of the 1837 Post Office Act were not too sound, for the Law Officers of the Crown warned the Postmaster-General that any court action would probably show that the *Great Western's* proprietors were within their rights in turning down the contract.

Much of this trouble was not really the Post Office's direct responsibility. There had for some time been a theory that the mail packets could usefully become a reserve defence force, and so they had been run by the Admiralty. Gradually it dawned on the Government that in times of crisis an even more important asset to the country's maritime and economic power would be a strong Merchant Navy, with the additional advantage that such encouragement would also produce great benefits in peacetime trade. It was, of course, the correct view. A few fast packets might have operated usefully as auxiliaries to the Navy in time of war, but the same amount of money as they would cost to build and run would pay far greater dividends as a subsidy to merchant shipowners. This applied particularly to the Atlantic routes, where a bitter war was being fought between rival companies and large amounts of capital were being sunk into the building of bigger and faster vessels.

A Nova Scotian named Samuel Cunard heard that the American mail contract had been rejected by the proprietors of the *Great Western*. He obtained this contract for seven years and got a subsidy of £55,000 from the Admiralty on 4 May 1839. The establishment of his steamship line marked a new era in transatlantic travel, and his four steamships, the *Britannia*, *Caledonia*, *Arcadia*, and *Columbia*, inaugurated a noble line of vessels carrying the Royal Mail to the New World.

The method of estimating the size of the subsidy favoured the shipowners once their vessels had been built and were earning money, and it grew by 1853 to the enormous sum of £853,140, three-quarters of which went to the Cunard, Royal Mail, and the P. & O. lines. Admittedly the ships had to sail at agreed times. with a regularity sometimes greater than that which seasonable trade warranted, and at high speed, but these factors hardly compensated the Post Office for the large sums allocated. Indeed. on some routes the contractors could quite fairly be asked to carry the mail as ordinary freight without loss to themselves.

When these changes were in the air, the overseas mail system was thrown into confusion by the outbreak of the Crimean War. This crisis proved how right the protagonists of subsidising merchant fleets rather than building potential warships had been. England had to fight a war at the other end of the Mediterranean, and she started to lose it because of the difficulties of supply. Then the fast passenger vessels built up by the mail subsidies came to the rescue. Twenty-eight of the best ships on the mail runs had been turned into troop and supply transports by December 1854. No steamers ran to Australia, the mail going by clipper instead. Britain indeed had reason to be grateful for the mail policy which had built up her Merchant Navy of fast commodious vessels.

The temporary use of sailing vessels on the Australian mail run was ended when the Admiralty signed a contract with the European and Australian Mail Company for the conveyance of a monthly mail via Suez. Britain paid half of the cost and Australia the other half, a system which was to be copied whenever possible in other parts of the Empire. The Australian mail had to go from Southampton to Melbourne in fifty-four days, and there were penalties for any delay beyond that time, whether the cause was storm or breakdown. The policy of letting the Admiralty control the mail packet service—by this time it merely meant seeing that the contracts were carried out—came to an end on 1 April 1860, when the Post Office once more took over entire control.

From that time the story of the packet service is one of continuous increase in the size and speed of mail ships, accompanied by continuous decrease in most Post Office payments for the services rendered. Parliament and the public had never cherished the principle of subsidies, and in the 'seventies the popular objection to subsidising ocean packet services, and the American mail service in particular, was expressed in very strong terms. An outcry for the abolition of the American mail subsidy was strengthened by the fact that an experiment of the United States Post Office in sending mails to the United Kingdom by the fastest available steamships taken up month by month with payment not by subsidy, but for the actual weight of correspondence carried, had proved successful, and it was persistently asked that a trial of the system should be made here. The contracts with the subsidised Companies (Cunard, Inman, and North German Lloyd) were accordingly terminated at the end of the year 1876, and the details of the American scheme were embodied in one formulated by the Post Office. It did not work well for many reasons, and the Post Office ultimately fell into the toils of what was popularly known as the " Liverpool Shipping Ring". It freed itself as a result of an action with the Cunard Steamship Company in which on 31 May 1889 a decree was pronounced to the effect:

> That the Postmaster-General is entitled to have all such post letter bags as he shall think fit received on board all or any vessels belonging to or chartered by the defendant Companies, outward bound from Liverpool or any other port or places in the United Kingdom, for conveyance upon such

ships or vessels to their respective ports or places of destination; and to have the same conveyed and delivered without delay on the arrival of such ships or vessels at such ports or places of destination.

Since the date of the decree the Post Office has had no similar difficulty in connection with the disposal of ship mails.

11

OVERLAND MAILS

THE great merchant routes which spread over Europe in the Middle Ages provided an overland postal service which enabled the traders of the Old World to communicate with one another. Letters could be sent to the Hanseatic towns, to almost every corner of France, and over the Alps to the prosperous banking and mercantile interests of Florence and Venice. From there it was possible to have them forwarded to Turkey and, no doubt, even farther into the East, along the great caravan routes to Asia. It is not the purpose of this book to trace the development of the Continental Posts, and indeed, after England's emergence as a nation concentrating on sea power to increase her trade and domination, the sea carriage of mails became of vastly greater importance than any of the overland routes through Europe, in some part of which hostilities were continually wrecking any organisation set up.

When a monopoly was granted to the East India Company in 1600 communication with the East and the Southern Hemisphere was virtually in the hands of that company. The vigour with which it pursued its trading policy provided a magnificent service of fast sailing ships which called at the Cape of Good Hope and Mauritius on the way to and from India. They carried mail— and carried it with greater speed and regularity than the packets run by the Post Office to the colonies in the New World. For this reason the Government was for a long time quite content to leave the responsibility in the hands of the East India Company. Then, under an Act approved by George III, the masters of every ship bound for the East Indies, the Cape, Ceylon, and Mauritius were compelled to carry mail free of charge on behalf of the Post Office.

By the beginning of the nineteenth century the volume of trade with India was enormous. Large numbers of British people lived out East, and the demand for fast communication outstripped even the Indian merchantmen's constant service between the two countries. A member of the Bengal Pilot Service, Thomas Waghorn, suggested in a letter to the Post Office a scheme for running a fast steamship between England and India. To help him maintain it he wanted a subsidy, and the difficulty here was that a special Act would have to be passed by Parliament excluding Waghorn's vessel from the general obligation to carry mails free. It was naturally rejected.

Waghorn must have been a persistent and resourceful man. Instead of accepting this as a final barrier to any speedier service, he began to investigate the possibilities of an overland mail via Egypt. In a second letter to the Post Office, he outlined his plans for testing the speed of the overland route in person. He proposed to leave London on 1 October, and see how quickly he could reach Bombay. He went via Paris, Trieste, across the Mediterranean to Alexandria, through Egypt to Suez, down the Red Sea by native boat and across the Indian Ocean by man-of-war, the *Thetis*. It was a remarkable effort merely to show how letters could be sent faster than on the Cape of Good Hope route, though it does not in itself seem to have caused much excitement at the time. However, Waghorn wrote to every influential person he could think of in both England and India, telling them of his exploit. He pointed out that the Post Office already sent mail as far as Malta. If these ships would continue their voyage to Alexandria, a service across Egypt could be comparatively easily organised, and then the East India Company could take over by running packets from Suez to Bombay. The average time of the voyage between England and India via the Cape was four months. In Waghorn's opinion, the Egyptian route would cut that time by half.

It was nine years before the Post Office and the East India Company agreed to spend the £100,000 a year necessary to run the overland route, but in 1837 it was inaugurated, with the intrepid Waghorn in charge of the Egyptian stage. At first the mails went by sea all the way from Falmouth to Alexandria, but after two years the distance and time were cut by sending them across France as far as Marseilles. This stage was a pioneer of the international overland mail service where correspondence belonging to another country had its own transit organisation in a foreign land. The Post Office ran its own coach from Calais to Paris. In the French capital it was transferred to the French mail coach, the sealed tin boxes (which could only be opened by cutting the metal plaques) occupying the inside of the vehicle normally used by passengers. The mail was loaded on to the waiting ship at Marseilles on the fifth day after despatch from the General Post Office in London. Much the same route was followed when France constructed her railways, and the Indian mail ran regularly on the French route until the Franco-Prussian War of 1870. The mail went in sealed vans under the personal care of a Post Office official, a unique example of one country allowing another to transport material through its territory without Customs examination or insistence of nationalistic rights of inspection, control, and so forth. Because of the cutting of communications with Paris in the war, the mail was then re-routed through Belgium and across Germany and Austria to Brindisi. Two years later Calais again became the entry port, and with the opening of the Mont Cenis Tunnel in the Alps, the Brindisi terminal was retained instead of reversion to Marseilles.

On the Egyptian stage the mails at first took five days. From Alexandria they went by native boat through the Mahmoudieh Canal and the Nile as far as Cairo, and then by camel or horses for two days as far as Suez, where the East India Company's vessel was waiting. In 1858 a railway was completed between Cairo and Suez and the mail, of course, went by it. When the Suez Canal was opened in 1869, there was a speed restriction to five miles an hour and vessels had to stop during the hours of darkness. For this reason the mails continued until 1888 to go through Egypt by rail; in that year the Suez Canal Company relaxed the restrictions about night travel, and the land route was abandoned.

The second great overland mail experiment in which the British Post Office became interested was the trans-Siberian mail service. In the latter years of the nineteenth century the project of a railway linking up East and West captured the imagination of many engineers. It was an ambitious idea, one of the great railway engineering projects of all time. In 1896, when the line was still incomplete, the Compagnie Internationale des Wagons-lits proposed that a plan for carrying mails from western Europe to Vladivostok on the Pacific coast should be investigated.

The Wagons-lits organisation calculated that it would need a subsidy of £81,000 a year to enable the service to be maintained. There were, of course, considerable British business interests in China which would benefit from such a mail service, but they were not numerous enough to justify a heavy subsidy, and the proposition was shelved. In addition, the eight weeks which it was calculated that letters would take because of the changes from trains to caravans and back again to trains hardly justified the official recognition of the route. It was not until 1903 that the Russian Post Office itself announced that a mail service would be operated over the Siberian route. The time from Moscow to Vladivostok was sixteen and a half days. After suspension in 1904 because of war in the Far East, the Russian Post Office announced in 1907 that the service would be twice a week from Moscow, the time of the transit thence being about twelve days to Vladivostok, and that for the time being no mails could be sent by the line running south from Harbin to Tientsin, Peking, and Hankow via Kouantchentsi. The use of the service was restricted to specially superscribed letters and postcards. An additional mail train once a week from Moscow was shortly afterwards put on. The route of Kouantchentsi was opened to mail traffic in October 1907, and afforded rapid transit for mails for places on the Chinese railways. In 1908 arrangements were made for transmitting mails for Shanghai (containing correspondence for other important districts of China) via Kouantchentsi and Dairen as well as via Vladivostok, by which route they had hitherto been sent exclusively. On the institution in 1909 of the Japanese packet service twice a week from Dalny, the Vladivostok route was given up for Shanghai mails. But the Siberian development was noteworthy because it really marked the arrival of a mail service to the four corners of the earth.

As the Post Office at the centre of a maritime group of nations,

in Britain, but among the officers of the postal services in the overseas possessions.   There was, however, the parallel of the era
preceding the Penny Post, and advocates who believed that cheap
rates would pay for themselves by increasing the popularity of
the Posts were not slow in coming forward.   Actually, any charge
of obstinacy to face facts cannot really be laid at the door of the
Government on this occasion.   In the disputes over the inland
Penny Post there had been irrefutable evidence that postal rates
were exorbitant, and there was the undeniable fact of a huge
population eager to write letters if they could afford to do so.   In
the controversy over charges for letters within the Empire, no
critic could bring forward evidence that private posts could carry
letters better or more cheaply than the official system; the distances
were enormous in places like the back blocks of Australia, and
tiny communities living many hundreds and even thousands of
miles from the main population centres had to be served, even
though the actual bag contained a mere score of letters and newspapers.

However reasonable those factors may be regarded to-day, they
did not restrain the principal advocate of Imperial Penny Postage,
John Henniker Heaton.   Born in 1848 in England, with more than
thirty years of experience of life in Australia, he started to badger
the Postmaster-General with questions and suggestions as soon as
he became M.P. for Canterbury in 1886.   The ghost of Robert
Wallace must have delighted in this apt pupil in the arts of
arousing public interest in the Posts by a never-ceasing flow of
pertinent questions in the House.   The Government benches were
not amused by the points which Heaton would raise in any and
every kind of debate, adroitly giving them a postal flavour so
that they were not ruled out of order.

Although he was at first told that the Colonies had no desire
for reduced charges and the General Post Office had no intention
of providing them, his constant criticism resulted in a technical
defeat of the Government and the Post Office, which in 1890
announced that letters for overseas would come down to $2\frac{1}{2}d.$ in
those cases where the rate exceeded this figure.

This was the year of celebrations of the Jubilee of the Penny
Posts, and the Postmaster-General was at pains to show at various

celebrations that the bad old days when Rowland Hill had to prod
the officials out of their lethargy had gone for good.   There was
certainly plenty of evidence that energy and initiative now
permeated the veins of the officials of St. Martin's-le-Grand, but
all the time, like a skeleton at the feast, was the critical spectre
of Henniker Heaton.   The latter kept on with his efforts, even
finding a patriotic Australian and Englishman to help him
guarantee the Post Office against loss if penny postage was
inaugurated.   Gradually Henniker Heaton won his battle.   The
penny postage came into operation for Canada on Christmas Day,
1898 (" to celebrate the birthday of the Prince of Peace ", as the
Postmaster-General told Queen Victoria), with the Cape Colony
in 1900, and New Zealand in 1901.   Letters to Australia went for
1*d*. in 1905 (but from Australia the 2*d*. rate was not lowered until
1911).   The final victory was the inauguration of penny postage
with the United States in 1908, a climax which meant that the
English-speaking nations of the world could write to one another
for 1*d*. wherever they were.   With a stamp purchased with this
humble coin a letter would cross 3,000 miles of ocean and another
3,000 miles of land to the people of San Francisco.   It would go
across 12,000 miles of sea to Sidney and thence over 1,000 miles
to Queensland.   The envelopes with the penny stamps and the
postmark of the capital, London, were borne into the North of
Canada by dog sleigh, through the tracks of the Himalayas in
north-west India by mule and runner.   Never had the posts been
so cheap, and it must be regretfully admitted they are never likely
to be so again.

12

THE TRAVELLING POST OFFICE

As early as 1838 the Post Office saw the advantages in sorting mail while travelling, and an Act passed in that year, regulating the use of railways for postal services, provided, among other things, that the railway company could be required to supply a special carriage for letter sorting. This facility greatly eased the work of the Postmasters along the route, for they no longer had to make up a large number of separate bags for each town on the route, and so the time when the collecting office closed could be still nearer the time of actual despatch.

The first travelling post office, with the Royal Arms on its central door, was running in the summer of 1838 on the Grand Junction line. It had two compartments, in one of which the coach guard sat, supervising the changing of the bags *en route*. In the second compartment the clerk stood at a small table, sorting the letters into pigeon-holes fixed on the wall.

On the exterior was a net which could be stretched outwards by an iron hoop and as the train passed a station the Postmaster dropped the bag of mail from his town into the net, while the guard simply threw the letters sorted for that area out of the window. As the train was going at less than twenty miles an hour this was not too difficult an operation.

This idea of sorting letters during the actual transit was first suggested by Frederick Karstadt, son of one of the Post Office surveyors, and it was first tried out in a converted horse-box. Then a permanent sorting carriage was built—quite a small affair only 16 feet long — and it also had an automatic device for

A MAIL COACH GUARD

SIR ROWLAND HILL

SECOND EDITION.

The Post Circular.

OR, ADVOCATE FOR A CHEAP, SWIFT, AND SURE POSTAGE.

No. 4. THURSDAY, APRIL 5, 1838. *Price* $2\frac{1}{2}$*d.*

The House of Commons now sitting is appointed—

"To inquire into the present rates and mode of charging postage, with a view to such a reduction thereof as may be made WITHOUT INJURY TO THE REVENUE; and for this purpose to examine specially into the mode recommended for charging and collecting postage, in a pamphlet published by Mr. Rowland Hill."

The plan proposed by Mr. Hill is:—

That all letters passing from one post town in the United Kingdom to another, be charged one penny for each half-ounce, to be paid in advance through the medium of stamped covers, on stamps or that letters should be stamped when delivered at the Post-offices.

This system would introduce uniformity and simplicity.—

An easy and cheap collection of the Revenue.—

Avoid a multiplicity of accounts kept at the Post-office.—

Save time in charging by pen and ink a varying rate on each letter, and in the delivery.

Avoid candle scrutiny into each letter to ascertain whether single or double as at present and consequent temptation to fraud.

The English Post-office Revenue has, during the last twenty years, slightly *diminished*.

The French Post-office Revenue has *increased more than half* since 1821.

The United States Post-office Revenue has more than *tripled* during the twenty years that ours has been nearly stationary.

The vast extent to which the trade of the country has increased within the last twenty years, must have been attended by a proportionate increase in mercantile correspondence, while the great spread of education, and increase of population during the same period, must have greatly augmented the correspondence of all kinds.

As the number of post letters sent through the Post-office, during the last twenty years, has not increased at all, it is manifest that the whole augmentation must have gone to swell the contraband conveyance.

The average of the present postage of a single letter (taking in all chargeable letters) is sixpence halfpenny.

The average cost of its actual carriage to *any* post town is about one-tenth of a penny.

The penny posts of large towns are very profitable, even though these pence have to be collected from house to house.

The average cost of managing the twopenny-post of London, notwithstanding the large allowance of weight, and the expensive manner in which the establishment is conducted, is only 34 per cent. on the receipts, or about two-thirds of a penny per letter.

The chargeable letters do not *weigh* more than about one-fourth of the whole mail.

These facts are stated that it may be seen upon what grounds the question of the reduction of postage is urged upon public attention,—but for a full view of this important subject, Mr. Rowland Hill's pamphlet, on Post-office reform, should be read, which is published by Charles Knight and Co., 22, Ludgate-street, London.

MR. ROWLAND HILL'S LETTERS TO LORD LICHFIELD.

LETTER III.—MEASURES CONTEMPLATED BY GOVERNMENT.

MY LORD—The changes which Government proposes to make in the Post-office Department, as appears by the statements of the Chancellor of the Exchequer, are, first, The reduction of the fourpenny postage to twopence; and second, The introduction of stamped covers to the twopenny-post department.

Your Lordship will be aware that this is an abandonment of the intention announced by Lord Duncannon in the House of Lords on the 30th of May last, which was as follows:—"My right hon. friend the Chancellor of the Exchequer proposes to reduce, to a certain extent, the charge on the transmission of letters, and although it is considered inexpedient to deprive persons of the opportunity of sending unpaid letters by the twopenny post, they will shortly be enabled to purchase envelopes which will carry them for *one penny each*."

This plan was in perfect accordance with the recommendation of the Commissioners of Post-office Inquiry (Lord Duncannon, Mr. Labouchere, and Lord Seymour), as appears from the following extract from their ninth report, page 7.—"We, therefore, propose to your Lordships that the distinction in the rates and districts which now applies to letters delivered by the twopenny and threepenny post shall not in any way affect correspondence transmitted under stamped covers; and that any letter not exceeding an ounce in weight shall be conveyed free within the metropolis, and the districts to which the town and country deliveries now extend, if enclosed in an envelope bearing a *penny stamp*.

This plan, it appears is now abandoned. The reduction is to be made on the fourpenny postage, while in the department of the twopenny post, there is to be no reduction whatever; the only change being the granting to the public an option to pay their postage as at present, or to make use of stamped covers, *charged according to the present rate*, viz., twopence for the twopenny post, and threepence for the threepenny post.

The reduction of the fourpenny postage to twopence, which, however, does not appear to be universal, is no doubt a boon to the public, nor should it be quarrelled with because it is given where it was neither most required nor most called for. Again it is valuable as an experiment on the effect of reduction; but as the change is in reduction only, and is not accompanied by any increased facility, more frequent opportunity, simplification of arrangements (with consequent economy), nor, in short, by any other improvements, even its failure would furnish no argument against my plan, though its success would strongly support one of the principles for which I contend. My dependence, however, is on a number of principles brought into harmonious operation, each aiding and strengthening all the others. They are, reduction of postage, increasing facilities, and simplification, with consequent economy in the mechanism of the Post-office.

If a trial of these separately should terminate in disappointment, this would be no sound reason against the trial of all conjointly, though were an experiment made under such disadvantages, to terminate in success, it might well be considered as establishing the substantive potency of the principle tried.

That the contemplated experiment will produce a considerable increase in the number of letters within the range of its operation, there can be no doubt, nor am I without hope that the revenue may even derive benefit from the change; but should this hope be disappointed, such failure will furnish no inference against the soundness of my plan.

With respect to the intended trial of the stamped covers, I must confess that I am entirely at a loss to conceive the scope of the experiment. The Chancellor of the Exchequer has announced, in the House of Commons, that it is the intention to try the stamped covers independently. Such an experiment, my Lord, must be futile: taken independently, stamped covers can be of little or no use, and will attract little or no attention from the public. I have already said that they are merely a means to an end.

To warrant so great a reduction of postage as I contemplate, there must be strict economy in the management of the Post-office. Strict economy requires extreme simplification, especially where the receipts are a vast number of small sums, and in the Post-office this extreme simplification requires payment in advance; but payment in advance cannot be exacted of the public without some compensation, and the Commissioners of Post-office Inquiry accordingly recommended in their report, when urging the partial adoption of my plan within the metropolitan district, that the stamped covers should be sold at the reduced price of *one penny*. And it ought carefully to be borne in mind that this lower charge is not an artificial contrivance for forcing stamped covers into use, but an equitable reduction consequent on the simple and economical arrangements to which their employment would lead.

As I have already said, my main security against loss to the Post-office revenue is on the increased number of letters. Still I am afraid that, were the postage in the metropolitan district to be reduced from 2*d.* to 1*d.*, without the establishment of payment in advance, and that by means of stamped covers, or some arrangement equally simple, the revenue might suffer by the change. The practical question, therefore, is between stamped covers at 1*d.* each, and payment on delivery at 2*d.* At the price of 2*d.* stamped covers would not be bought; the payment of a penny on delivery would not sustain the revenue.

To conclude, the reduction in the fourpenny postage, which is not a partial but a garbled trial of my plan, though its failure will weaken no one of my positions may, by its success, demonstrate in the principle of reduction a potency beyond what I claim for it. Should the trial of stamped covers on the plan now unfortunately contemplated issue in success, the world will indeed see a paradox—an effect without a cause. Were such an experiment merely useless it might pass without comment; but its inevitable failure may produce no small mischief. An apparent trial of a plan may easily be confounded with a real one; and though I am sure nothing could be further from the intentions of the Chancellor of the Exchequer, yet had the aim been to throw unfair discredit on the plan, it would have been difficult to devise a better mode of proceeding.

I have, &c.,

ROWLAND HILL.

REMARKS ON VARIOUS MODES PROPOSED FOR FRANKING LETTERS, UNDER MR. ROWLAND HILL'S PLAN OF POST-OFFICE REFORM.

In suggesting any method of improvement, it is only reasonable to expect that what are supposed to be its advantages over any existing system, or in opposition to others that have been, or may be proposed, will be explicitly stated.

Therefore, if Mr. Hill's plan of a uniform rate of postage,—and that all postages are to be paid by those sending letters, *before* they are deposited in the respective Post-offices,—become the law of the land, I conceive that the most simple and economical mode of making such an arrangement would be by *slips*, prepared somewhat similar to the specimen herewith shewn.

With this view, and in the hope that Mr. Hill's plan may soon be carried into operation, I would suggest that sheets of stamped slips should be prepared at the Stamp-office (on a paper made expressly for the purpose), with a devise on each from a die or cut resembling that on newspapers; that the *sheets* so printed or stamped should then be rubbed over on the back with a strong solution of gum, or other adhesive substance, and (when thoroughly dry) issued by the Stamp-office to town and country distributors, to stationers and others, for sale in sheets or singly, under the same laws and restrictions now applicable to those selling bill or receipt stamps, so as to prevent, as far as practicable, any fraud on the revenue.

Merchants and others, whose correspondence is extensive, could purchase these slips in quantities; cut them singly, and affix one to a letter by means of wetting the back of the slip with a sponge or brush, just with as much facility as applying a wafer, for which, in many cases (for instance circulars), the slip might answer; while either a wafer or wax may also be applied at the option of the writer. Others, requiring only one or two slips at a time, could purchase them along with sheets of paper at stationers' shops. The *weight only* regulating the rate of postage in all cases, so as a stamp may be affixed according to the scale determined on.

Again to prevent the possibility of these being used a *second time*, it should be made imperative on postmasters to put the Post-office town stamp (as represented on one of the specimens) across the slip or postage stamp.

General Postage.	General Postage.
NOT EXCEEDING ONE OUNCE.	NOT EXCEEDING HALF AN OUNCE.
Twopence.	One Penny.

It appears to me that the advantages to be derived from this plan of slips, over envelopes or stamped sheets of paper, must be obvious. The writers of letters will not be confined to any length of letter, or mode of folding it, in which they must often be guided by circumstances,—the time requisite for affixing the slip will scarcely exceed that of inserting a wafer—and the weight of it little, if any thing more.

What appears to me to be objectionable to the use of envelopes—specimens of which we have seen exhibited in public places,—are, *first*, the expense which there must be in paper and printing, not less, in my opinion, than 25 per cent. on the proposed rate of postage—consequently an unnecessary sacrifice of the revenue; *secondly*, the various sizes requisite to suit all dimensions of paper and methods of folding letters; and *lastly*, the great increase of weight and bulk they would unavoidably occasion; for, if Mr. Hill's calculations should prove nearly correct, namely, that, by his proposed reduction of postage there would be, in consequence, an increase of letters to *six times* their present number, the result would therefore be, by using envelopes, to increase the size and weight of the daily correspondence to about *nine times* what it is just now.

Again, as to *stamped sheets* of paper, to answer for correspondence by post, such seems to me to be objectionable in so far as few writers of letters can calculate on *perfecting* or completing the letter on the sheet they first commence to write on; so that in numerous instances a sacrifice would unavoidably be made to the writer, both of the paper and stamp, should a second or third be required.

Taking all these disadvantages into consideration, the use of stamped slips is certainly the most preferable system; and, should others who take an interest in the proposed reform, view it in the same light as I do, it remains for them to petition Parliament to have such carried into operation.

JAMES CHALMERS.

4, Castle-street, Dundee,
8th February, 1838.

[Mr. Hill's plan of obtaining payment in advance does not limit itself to the use of *stamped covers*. To meet every possible case, Mr. Hill proposes sheets or half-sheets, of various sizes and weights, stamped,—likewise the use of stamps which may be attached as Mr. Chalmers suggests, or when neither are to be procured, that the letter upon payment of its postage may be stamped at the Post-office. Mr. Chalmers' objection that one sheet may not hold all the writer wishes to say, might be removed by the writer's completing his letter on a separate piece of paper, and inclosing it in the sheet—taking care that the prescribed weight was not trespassed on.]

An April, 1838, issue of "The Post Circular," one of the many publications avidly read during the agitation for the Penny Post. This issue mentions Rowland Hill's suggestion of pre-paid stamps, in the footnote at the bottom right-hand corner.

LEFT: The cover of the famous Post Office Act of 1656, issued by the Lord Protector in 1657. RIGHT: An official notice that changed the letter communication system of the world: the Post Office regulations for the Penny Post issued in January.

POST OFFICE REGULATIONS.

ON AND AFTER THE **10th January,** a Letter not exceeding HALF AN OUNCE IN WEIGHT, may be sent from any part of the United Kingdom, to any other part, for ONE PENNY, if paid when posted, or for TWO PENCE if paid when delivered.

THE SCALE OF RATES,

If paid when posted, is as follows, for all Letters, whether sent by the General or by any Local Post, **One Penny.**

Not exceeding ½ Ounce	....	**Twopence.**
Exceeding ½ Ounce, but not exceeding 1 Ounce	**Fourpence.**
Ditto	1 Ounce .... 2 Ounces	**Sixpence.**
Ditto	2 Ounces .... 3 Ounces	**Eightpence.**

and so on; an additional Two-pence for every additional Ounce. With but few exceptions, the WEIGHT is limited to Sixteen Ounces.

If not paid when posted, double the above Rates are charged on Inland Letters.

COLONIAL LETTERS.

If sent by Packet Twelve Times, if by Private Ship Eight Times, the above Rates.

FOREIGN LETTERS.

The Packet Rates which vary, will be seen at the Post Office. The Ship Rates are the same as the Ship Rates for Colonial Letters.

As regards Foreign and Colonial Letters, there is no limitation as to weight. All sent outwards, with a few exceptions, which may be learnt at the Post Office, must be paid when posted as heretofore.

Letters intended to go by Private Ship must be marked "*Ship Letter.*"

Some arrangements of minor importance, which are omitted in this Notice, may be seen in that placarded at the Post Office.

No Articles should be transmitted by Post which are liable to *injury by being stamped,* or by being crushed in the Bags.

It is particularly requested that all Letters may be *fully and legibly addressed, and posted as early as convenient.*

January 7th, 1840.

By Authority.—J. Hartnell, London.

AN ACT
FOR THE
SETLING
OF THE
POSTAGE
OF
ENGLAND,
SCOTLAND and IRELAND.

At the Parliament begun at *Westminster* the 17th Day of *September,* Anno Domini 1656.

LONDON:
Printed by *Henry Hills* and *John Field,* Printers to His Highness the Lord Protector. 1657.

exchanging mail bags *en route*. The basic design was by John Ramsey, an officer of the Missing Letters Branch, and an improved device which is basically the same as that in use today was built in 1848. It was another effort by a Post Office employee, John Dicker, a mail coach inspector. The regular run of the first travelling post office was quite short—from London to Bletchley, Buckinghamshire, where Watling Street, one of the country's busiest coach roads, crossed the line. Then on 1 October 1838, the service was extended so that the coach went right through from London to Preston. There were two runs daily, one at 11 a.m. and another at 8.30 p.m.

Before the advent of the travelling post office some 800 separate bags were made up for the trains and mail coaches serving the route from London to the Midlands and the north-west; afterwards this number was reduced to fifty-one on the outward mail and forty-four on the inward run. As more railways were opened up, other travelling post offices were put into service. By 1852 they were running between Rugby and Newcastle-on-Tyne, Exeter and Bristol, Gloucester and Tamworth, and Chester and Holyhead. Then in 1860 a travelling post office was added to the Continental mail service between London and Dover.

Just before this the first mail trains were also running. The Post Office had a legal right to demand special trains as well as the carriage of mails at the maximum speed of any train on the system. The Limited Mail — a train run primarily for postal services, but permitted to carry passengers—steamed out for the first time on 1 February 1859 for Scotland. It consisted of three sorting carriages and three postal vans, in addition to luggage trucks and carriages.

The first special mail train ran in 1885 on the old London and North-Western and Caledonian railways. This train was devoted entirely to the mail service for towns between London and Aberdeen and ran in both directions.

Until the Irish Free State came into being, the Post Office was, of course, responsible for the distribution of mails in Ireland as well as Great Britain. The first Irish travelling post office ran between Dublin and Cork on New Year's Day 1855, and vastly speeded up

6

the night mail from England and the north of the country to the towns in the south and west. Five years later the time was still further cut by the use of sorting offices on the mail packets running between Holyhead and Kingstown. It is interesting to note, by the way, that the tradition of the old mail coach guard lasted for a very long time; until 1857 the men who received and despatched the bags at the railway stations were called guards.

To-day the coaches keep between 400 and 600 officials busy according to the time of the year, and they cover nearly 2½ million miles a year. There are now four Post Office trains, two of them the largest of their kind in the world. The Up Special from Aberdeen to Euston covers the journey between 3.30 p.m. and 4.0 a.m., and on its journey deals with an average of 1,800 bags of mail. Her sister train, the Down Special, leaves Euston at 8.30 p.m. and arrives at Aberdeen at 8.15 a.m. The Western Region's two Specials run between Penzance and Paddington (and *vice versa*), covering the 305-mile journey in just over nine hours.

The busy scene at any of the terminal stations half an hour before the Mail Specials are due to leave is well worth a visit. Every minute red Post Office vans are arriving in the station yard, while still more mountains of mail bags are delivered by the conveyors from the Post Office underground railway. Quickly and methodically, the bags are divided into sections and loaded into the appropriate sorting coach. Long before the train starts these bags are opened by the sorters already at work—there may be as many as eighty of them behind the almost windowless walls of the carriages—and the job continues steadily as with very little whistle-blowing and none of that familiar banging of doors and last-minute farewells of the usual express, the Night Mail goes on its way. An even better place to appreciate the activity which comes to the Post Office while most of the public is asleep is to spend an hour or so on Crewe Station. This great junction, which gives direct connections with every area of Great Britain, is used by trains connecting every part of the country, and is the principal centre for the transit of mails which do not come from, or have to be delivered to, the Metropolis.

The modern picking-up and setting-down apparatus is a common enough feature of our main line railway systems, though, in the very nature of its use during the " wee sma' hours ", very few people have seen it work. Those enthusiasts who have risen early on a summer's morning to watch the exchange of pouches are usually disappointed. The whole thing happens so quickly as the train dashes through at more than forty miles an hour that it would need a slow-motion cine-camera really to appreciate the simple, fool-proof action which automatically takes place.

The stationary device beside the railway line consists of a standard with a short swivelling arm at the top. Alongside it is the receiving net. When the mail train is due, the pouches containing the bags of mail are hung from the arm, which is turned at right angles to the track, and the net is opened to receive the mail bags from the train.

Inside the special coaches on the mail train equipped for transfer of pouches at speed a wide door is opened and two arms are swung outwards carrying the outgoing pouches a few hundred yards ahead of the exchange point. As soon as this is done a bell rings as a warning to sorters passing through the coaches to keep clear. The whole operation for the actual despatch and reception of the pouches is automatic and almost simultaneous. The outstretched train net releases the bags hanging from the standard arm, and the two supports from the carriage throw the outgoing pouch into the wayside net. The faster the train is going the more certain is the device to operate. In any event, the twenty or so operations of this kind which take place every night on an important night mail become as routine as sorting letters to the staff. If a failure occurred it would be due to mis-timing of the preparations by the officer on the train, but this is so unlikely that it ranks with the sensation of the Guardsman dropping his rifle at the ceremony of Trooping the Colour. In other words, officially it just does not happen!

Nevertheless, the operation does demand considerable skill and great knowledge of the line despite the help of white warning boards. Pouches have to be hung out at the correct moment; not too early, in case some projection, such as a tunnel or bridge, might be in the way; and not too late so that the distance decreasing at nearly a mile a minute is insufficient to get everything ready. It will be appreciated that the apparatus officer must always be a veteran of the route. He develops the uncanny instinct of a blind man to recognise places by sound. The clatter of points at a junction, the momentary roar of a tunnel, the echo reflected by the canopy of a tiny station, or the hollow sound as the train crosses a bridge are all etched in his memory, so that, irrespective of time, and certainly without the help of any visual evidence on a pitch black night deep in the country when every lamp is out and the whole world seems asleep, he will be able to say exactly where the train is, though maybe there is any spot on a 400-mile journey from which to choose.

Mention must also be made here of the Post Office tube railway, which was authorised for construction in 1913 at a cost estimated at £964,000 over the three years needed for its completion. When war broke out in August 1914, only a small amount of work had been undertaken, costing £20,000, but after some hesitancy it was decided to proceed with the work, the excavated tunnel coming in most useful for the storage of valuables from the museums and art galleries of London. Through the problems of war and the economic troubles afterwards, as well as unexpected engineering difficulties, the railway took thirteen years to complete, and cost more than £1¾ millions by the time it was opened for service in 1927.

The line runs from Whitechapel to Paddington, with intermediate stations at Liverpool Street, the General Post Office, Mount Pleasant, Holborn, Wimpole Street, and Oxford Street. This double-track railway, extending more than six and a half miles under London, is unique in the world, and few people in London who boast of the network of sewers, subways, railway tubes, and deep air raid shelters which honeycomb the foundations of the country's capital know that there is also this system some 80 feet below the streets. The trains run on tracks with a 2-foot gauge, and are entirely automatic, carrying no driver or guard. During the evening peak hours the service is at three-minute intervals and the running speed is thirty-five miles an hour. Lifts, conveyors, and chutes obviate most of the man-handling of the mail bags to and from the surface offices, and about 35,000 mail

bags of parcels and letters are handled every twenty-four hours.
The advantages of the Post Office tube in peacetime are
innumerable. Mail can go from East London to West London in
twelve minutes, against the thirty-five minutes which is a fair
average road time for the similar journey even when congestion is
not serious, and the lack of hold-ups through weather or
unpredictable conditions like road repairs, diversions, and so on
enables much tighter timing to be followed to catch the mail trains.
In the war, when the trains could run untroubled by raids and
black-out, the tube really proved its worth. In terms of money,
the railway cost, in 1948-9, £80,406 for maintenance and deprecia-
tion. This was 0·1 per cent. of the total expenditure on postal
services and certainly a splendid investment.

13

PARCELS BY POST

ALTHOUGH a parcel post system had been suggested in 1839, it was turned down by the Government during the general study of the Penny Post scheme. It is probably well that they did reject any national service at a uniform rate, as even a modest popularity would have necessitated more stage coaches, much heavier payments to the railways then in use, and an increase of staff at the sorting offices. Such a service would have still further aggravated the decrease in profits which so alarmed some officials when the income and expenditure of the first twelve months of operation under the Penny Post system were balanced.

In 1848, as a previous chapter told, a compromise was reached with the introduction of the book post, and with the worries which beset Rowland Hill in the next few years he himself did little to hasten the arrival of a parcel post. Some of the advocates of such a service glibly suggested a 1*d*. charge, taking into account none of the expenses incurred in transporting a parcel as compared with a letter. Some European countries had a parcel post by the 'seventies, and at the Paris Postal Conference of 1880 a definite arrangement for an international system was put forward. Britain attended this meeting, but was in the invidious position, as a pioneer of mail organisation, in being unable to co-operate because of the non-existence of a British inland parcel post. The tardiness was not all on the side of the Post Office. The Postmaster-General of that time, Henry Fawcett, a man who did not let his blindness prevent him from becoming one of the great holders of his office in recent times, was anxious to get a parcel post started. The stumbling-block was the price the railways wanted to exact. For two years the negotiations continued, the result being that the railway companies should receive eleven-twentieths of the postage on all parcels sent by rail. Although carriage of bulky and fragile packets might certainly be more expensive than the transport of letters, the cost could certainly not be anything like this proportion of the total fee charged to the sender, and the arrangement, a triumph for the railways, was an intolerable burden to the Post Office. However, the agreement became law on 18 August 1882, and a little less than twelve months later a parcel post was in operation. Charges were very reasonable: 3d. up to 1 lb., 6d. between 1 and 3 lb., 9d. between 3 and 5 lb., and 1s. from 5 to the maximum of 7 lb. It was an immediate success, 1¾ millions of parcels being sent every month. In the following financial year, 1884-5, the number increased to nearly 2 millions a month. It was unfortunate that the letter-carriers, who were henceforth called postmen, had to bear the burden of parcel delivery without extra pay. The reason must be that the £250,000 which the Post Office received in the first year from parcel postage did not cover the expenditure, and while the gross revenue increased by £705,467, the net revenue dropped by £86,000. Parcels could be up to 3 feet 6 inches in length, or 6 feet in length and girth combined, and the postman setting out with a load of parcels of this sort must have literally staggered under the burden.

Nevertheless, the service was steadily expanded. On 1 July 1885 it was possible to send a parcel to Gibraltar, Aden, India, and Egypt, with the highest cost (to India) at the modest rate of 1s. per pound. In the months that followed, parcel services were opened with many other countries as well. In May 1886, when Lord Wolverton was Postmaster-General, the maximum weight of inland parcels was raised to 11 lb., and the rates changed so that, generally speaking, they gave a lower postal charge. The number of inland parcels rose by 7 millions a year, and there were 394,000 parcels passing to and from foreign countries.

All this time the railways were exacting their heavy charges and making an extremely good thing out of it. Henry Raikes, who had succeeded Lord Wolverton as Postmaster-General in 1886, thought of a method of retaining some of the money received on parcel postage. The Act of 1882 had made the proviso that the railways received their share on parcels carried by rail—not on all parcels. Consequently, there was a loophole by returning to the mail coach era. The first coach ran between London and Brighton on 1 June 1887. It provided a night service which was entirely adequate for morning delivery on the Sussex coast and in the towns along the Brighton Road. Better vehicles and a carefully organised system of stages enabled the old-time Tudor speeds of seven miles an hour to be bettered—by one mile. It seemed a retrograde step to carry the mail at eight miles an hour when trains were averaging forty miles an hour or more, but the all-important question of cost more than justified the road service. Soon the coaches were running on several other roads, even as far as Manchester. They worked well until the first motor vehicles were put on the roads in 1898. One likes to think that the utter defeat of the mail coach in the 'forties was, after all, not so complete as it had then appeared, and that for nine years the horse came back into its own.

At the turn of the century, when the motor lorries first helped with the parcels post, the number of parcels passing through the inland Post was 67,885,000. To-day it is more than 214,000,000. In the earlier period the foreign parcels service carried just over 2,000,000. Now it exceeds 22,000,000.

The parcel post service between Britain and America had an unusual scheme at the outset. The official service started after some years of negotiation in April 1905, but the U.S. postal authorities could not agree about the accounting system necessary for those parcels which passed through the United States, nor on such matters as insurance against loss and provision of express delivery facilities. These services, and in addition a greater toleration as regards maximum weight, had been provided by the American Express Company, and for a time both official and semi-official services ran simultaneously. The official system was cheaper for parcels of less than 4 lb. 6 oz. in weight, but in actual operation the American Express carried slightly more in the first year, 1,692 parcels against the 1,629 of the official service in a typical month. The real reason for this double service by official and semi-official methods was that the United States did not have an inland parcel post until 1912, though there was, of course, a number of well-run private parcel-forwarding companies in operation long before this.

To assist trade, special rates for overseas letters containing samples had been started in the eighteenth century, but it was not until 1862 that the official foreign pattern post was established, with an inland service in the following year. It was intended for trade patterns and samples only, and no articles sent in this way could have any intrinsic value. Packets weighing 4 oz. and under went for 3d., and even bulky samples up to 24 oz. paid only 1s. 6d. About half a million packets were posted in the first year, and this total was doubled in the following twelve months. Of undoubted value to traders (as it still is in the case of overseas business), the steady reduction in rates to ½d. for every 2 oz. in 1870 made the sample post very attractive indeed—regrettably to people who were certainly not issuing samples and patterns. Such tricks as posting odd stockings on separate days, and even parts of machinery, were not easy to check without an army of investigators. The pattern post was abolished in 1871, when the letter postage rates were lowered. It had another ten years of revived existence from 1887 to 1897, when the Diamond Jubilee celebrations again brought general postage reductions that made an inland pattern post redundant. Sample post facilities were re-introduced on 23 May 1932, in the inland service.

Another packet service which is of benefit to trade is the C.O.D. system. More than 3 millions are now handled every year. The description of the service as a benefit to traders needs qualification: it assists some traders and is alleged to hurt others. The reason for the criticism is that a local trader thereby receives direct competition from large mail order houses, which can offer unbeatable competition through bulk purchase and low profit margins. This is not quite true, for even if the postman bearing the C.O.D. packet is regarded as a salesman of the mail order house, he will come only if the customer has spent time and money in writing for the goods he brings, and he will charge for his trouble. However, retailers' protests against any such system, which was running in other countries at least sixty years ago, effectively prevented the Post Office starting any scheme, though they were anxious to do so, for many years—in the case of the inland ser-

vice until after the First World War. Eventually the Post Office
and the retailers reached a compromise by restricting C.O.D. posts
to overseas countries. The plan was announced by Lord Derby,
the then Postmaster-General, in 1904. It was high time that the
traders gave way, for German merchants were flooding the world
with quaintly worded catalogues of goods which persuaded those
in the outposts of the Empire to send their orders to Hamburg
instead of Birmingham, and Berlin instead of London. France
was also busily engaged in this overseas trading by post, and
British retail houses specialising in direct sales to overseas
customers were losing goodwill as well as money.

The overseas C.O.D. service finally started in 1908 and rapidly
extended to a large number of countries. In the first full years of
the system 29,380 packets were despatched and 804 received.
To-day the position is reversed, and in 1948-9 only 2,000 were
sent abroad while 158,000 were received. Compared with the
other branches of the postal service, the C.O.D. system is very
small, but it is just another example of the way in which every
facility which has a demand is met.

14

WITH EXTRA CARE

DAMAGED or lost parcels and registered letters, though a small proportion of the enormous value of the items handled, represent a heavy financial burden to the Post Office. In 1948-9, for example, compensation was paid to the public to the total of £229,000, and a large proportion of this sum (£136,000) concerned unregistered parcels. Even though the cheap facility of registration is available, the public persists in a " penny wise pound foolish " policy of saving the cost of registration.

From the earliest days the sanctity and safety of the mails was kept to the fore. There were, however, as we have read in earlier chapters, considerable risks of robbery during transit before the advent of the mail coach with its well-armed guard, and even the fact that robbing the Posts was a capital offence up to 1835 (the last man executed for letter-stealing was hanged on 13 February 1832) did not prevent highwaymen and footpads risking their lives in order to rob the mail. Very often these robberies were easily carried out because of the cowardice of the post boys or even with their co-operation in return for a share of the spoils. It was really the desire to ensure a safe method of postage for money that started the Post Office on the road which has to-day made it one of the country's biggest bankers as well as inaugurating the money order and postal order system.

The first rough-and-ready method to ensure safe transit was to cut cheques and negotiable documents in half, sending one section on one day and the other on the next. This was popular up to the time that the money order system was first considered in 1791, and even to-day Treasury note serial numbers are printed twice for this reason. Mr. Gosnell, an accountant of Crutched Friars, in the city of London, put forward two schemes, one of which was virtually that used to-day. The Post Office was enthusiastic about it, but its legal advisors doubted whether the Parliamentary Acts authorising the monopoly of mail-carrying also permitted the setting up of a kind of banking organisation, and nothing could be done officially. If the Postmaster-General could not run a money system, as it was called, there was nothing to prevent him advertising such a service and encouraging the Clerks of the Road to start yet another sideline; they already had the profitable newsagency business. More than that, the Secretary of the Post Office and other officials had a franking privilege. With their signatures on the money letter advices, these could go through the Posts free, and materially reduce the running costs. The Clerks saw the point, and went ahead with the scheme.

The Clerks of the Road had considerable ready money at their disposal and the payment of the cash on the surrender of the money letter by the recipient presumably did not offer great problems. In any event, the system started on 1 October 1792, theoretically restricted to a maximum of five guineas per letter, but in practice available for larger sums. The commission was 6d. in the £1, shared equally by the sender and the recipient. A few months later, on money letters from London, the commission was reduced to 4d., but in the general increase of prices during the latter stages of the Napoleonic wars the rate went up to 8d. for all orders, and there were stamp duties as well. Until someone thought of printing the money letters on a sheet with a blank space below it, the pay slip and covering note counted as a double letter, so that there were heavy postal charges on top of all the other costs.

As one reason for the money letter service had been to provide a method for the large number of troops mobilised on the coast to guard against invasion to send pay to their families, it will be seen that the costs of sending even £1 any great distance were very heavy, and no doubt many of the soldiers preferred to risk sending coins by some other method sooner than pay out these heavy charges. As we shall see, the risk was quite small by one popular method.

By 1797 about 11,800 money letters were being issued from

London, but the scheme was running at a loss. The Clerks of the Road found that they were £298 out of pocket on nearly six years of operation, and they threw in their hand. It was probably unwise of them, for they had started with only £1,000 capital, and with the privileges tacitly given them by the Post Office a little more energy and patience would have built up a profitable business. This must have been the opinion of the senior Clerk, named Barnes, who invited Daniel Stow, an official of the Inland Office, and a man named Slater to join him in a private venture. They ran their business for thirty years without interference and presumably made a success of it, though as it was an entirely private scheme no figures of the annual turnover can now be discovered. Then a Government committee investigated the Money Order Office, as it was then called, and they voiced their profound disapproval at the lack of official control. The remaining founder-partner at that time was Daniel Stow, and it was ordered that no new partners should be admitted. Stow died in 1836, and the survivor, a man named Watts, was bought out with a pension of some £400 a year in 1838. The same compensatory method was used in the case of a Clerk of the Road in Ireland who started an Irish money order office in 1831, and the field was clear to inaugurate an official system on 6 December 1838. Some idea of the size of the business which had been built up by that time by Barnes and his colleagues is forthcoming from the figures for the first year under the Post Office: 188,000 money orders were issued in 1839. When the rates were reduced the following year to 3d. on orders up to £2 and 6d. from £2 to £5, the number rose to 587,000.

The general increase in letter-writing which then occurred through the popularity of the Penny Post nearly trebled this figure in 1841. Thirty years later still further reductions in commission were made so that it was possible to buy a money order value 10s. for 1d. commission. The business became very large reaching 18,000,000 orders handled in 1877-8, but it was not profitable at these low charges, and the Post Office was losing £10,000 a year on running it. A couple of years later postal orders for small sums provided the solution. To-day the money order is steadily returning to favour, partly because it is used by

Government departments for certain payments to the public. In its various forms — telegraph, foreign, and transits from one country to another—more than 21,000,000 are now handled every year. They bring an income of about £600,000 to the Post Office revenue.

A foreign money order system was yet another of the ambitious plans of Rowland Hill. He drafted a plan for it as early as 1843, but no active steps were taken until 1849, when there was a considerable agitation to provide a money order service for the benefit of the many emigrants going out to New Zealand. Once again the financial difficulties seemed too great and the scheme was shelved.

In 1855 the difficulties experienced by the many civilians out in the Crimean theatre of war brought the matter to a head. The War Office sent the troops' money home to their families, but the nurses, contractors' assistants, seamen, and other civilians had no such facility. There were many cases of real hardship as a result, which Florence Nightingale solved in her usual practical manner of getting wrongs put right by sending the money in lump sums herself. At one period she was despatching £50 a week on behalf of civilians in the Crimea. No doubt she used her energies to get this injustice put right, as she did so many more serious examples of mismanagement. By the beginning of 1856 the Army Post Office was selling money orders to the value of £1,600 a week, and by the end of the war £106,000 had been sent home in this way. The system thus built up remained after hostilities were over, mainly providing a service for the military and naval stations in the Mediterranean. Between 1858 and 1867 the Imperial money order service was extended to cover most of the Empire, an inestimable boon to the hundreds of thousands of emigrants who went to every part of the Empire in those years. Gradually the system was extended to Europe and then still further afield. But the Imperial and foreign money order has, unhappily, never become universal like the Post, and with the present currency troubles which beset the majority of nations, including our own, this must remain an ambition for the future.

Returning to the early days of the money letter, the alternative methods of sending valuables deserve examination. It is small wonder that the troops persisted in entrusting actual coins to the Posts, despite warnings that the movement of the coach might rub a hole in the cover, for the Post Office provided an excellent service without charge to look after such letters. The sender had simply to take his letter to the postal clerk with an explanation that it contained valuables and the latter thereupon marked it in red ink, entering details of it on a sheet of paper, in which the letter was then wrapped. This bill had to be receipted by the postmaster at the other end. No charge whatever was made for the service beyond the normal one of double rates because of the enclosure. Many people would put a trinket or small coin in any letter which they particularly desired should be safely received. When the various postal arrangements were being investigated in 1838, it was stated that 110,000 letters a year were being registered without charge in this way at the London Inland Office alone.

The Post Office had by this time obtained authorisation to charge a fee for this service, but it was not anxious to bring it into operation, because automatically the fee would necessitate compensation for loss or theft, and as there were no means of estimating what this might total in any legal damages, the innovation had not been adopted. In 1838, however, the Treasury said that compensation should be limited to £5 and cases judged on their merits. All the plans to bring the registration system into force were again abandoned in view of the imminence of the Penny Post. The large increase in the number of letters which Rowland Hill envisaged would make special handling of a proportionate increase in registered letters impracticable. Not only was the new scheme abandoned, but the older free system of safeguarding was stopped as well. The inevitable result was a rise in the number of petty thefts of letters which clearly contained coins or valuables. Once again the need for registration became pressing, and on 6 January 1841 the fee was set at 1s. Only sixty registered letters left London daily at this high rate.

Large numbers of valuables were still going through the ordinary posts to save the fee, a constant temptation to the clerks and letter-carriers. Thereupon it was suggested that coin or jewellery be compulsorily registered, a move resisted by Rowland Hill, who also put forward an alternative plan for an immediate reduction in the registration fee to an interim fee of 6d., eventually dropping to 2d. This seemed a good idea but for one point: the Post Office had been busily building up the money order service, and the new charges would undercut this service, so that very few people indeed would trouble to buy a £1 money order for 6d. if they could register a sovereign for 2d. The quarrel about the registration fee was one of the causes of Rowland Hill's dismissal by Peel in 1842 from his post at the Treasury, and he had to wait six years, until he was back in the Post Office as Secretary in 1848, before the 6d. registration fee came into force. At the time of the change the number of registered letters was still low—only about 300 a day from London.

In 1862 the legal niceties of compulsory registration of letters containing coins, watches, jewellery, and uncut banknotes were settled in favour of the Post Office, and at this stage also the registration fee was decreased to 4d. There was an immediate rise in the number of registrations, by this time available for many places abroad, to a total of 2,000,000 a year. Since then there has been a continual expansion of the precautions provided for valuable letters and parcels, including a system of insurance which was introduced in May 1886. This idea proved expensive to run and was largely abandoned a year later in favour of a general registration system with its limits of compensation according to the fee paid which we now know. The 2,000,000 registered letters which were sent in the first year of the cheap 4d. rate have risen to 123,000,000 at the present time, while the registered and insured parcels total 35,000,000. Every one of these items has its slip and counterfoil, an example of the care which organisation can provide for one item out of millions. The registered letter with its crossed blue lines (a relic of the days when each packet was tied with blue tape and sealed) is a remarkable feature of the Posts.

The postal order was one of the innovations of the Post Office identified with the term of office of Henry Fawcett. They were first issued on New Year's Day 1881, as a cheaper method of handling small sums than that provided by the money order service. The idea was immediately successful, some 4½ millions being sold in the first year, representing a sum of £2,000,000. For the comparative figures of to-day, the post-war figures are

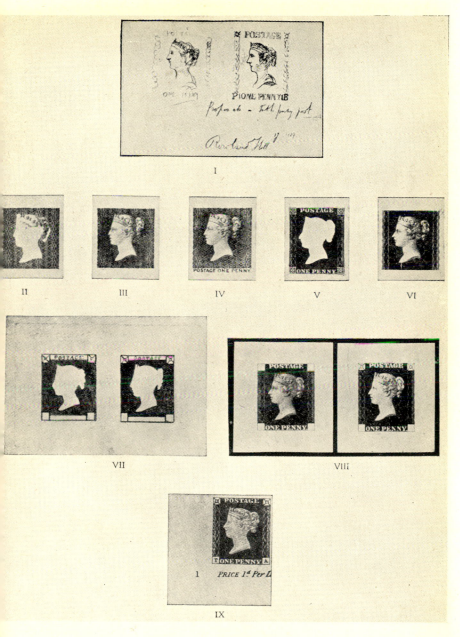

I

II   III   IV   V   VI

VII   VIII

IX

he evolution of the design of the Penny Black. At the top is the original sketch
made by Rowland Hill for the artist's guidance.

OLD ORIGINAL.

TOP: The original die used for the Penny Black. RIGHT: The Wyon medal on which the head of Queen Victoria for the Penny Black stamp was based. It set the style for stamp design which has continued ever since the world over.

PROOF OF THE FIRST PENNY PLATE

MADE IN APRIL 1840 BEFORE THE INSCRIPTION AND CHECK LETTERS WERE ADDED.

SIGNED ON THE BACK BY ROWLAND HILL.

A philatelist's dream: the proof of the first plate of the famous Penny Black, made in April, 1840, before the inscription and check letters were added. In the possession of the G.P.O., it is signed on the back by Rowland Hill.

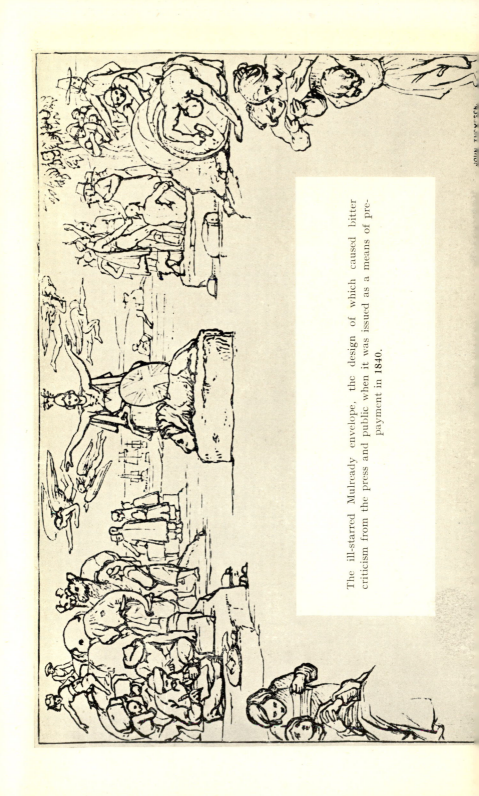

The ill-starred Mulready envelope, the design of which caused bitter criticism from the press and public when it was issued as a means of pre-payment in 1840.

422,000,000, bringing an income from the poundage charges of more than £2⅔ millions, of which a large proportion comes from football pools.

The 1881 orders ranged from 1*s.* to £1, the poundage being ½*d.* up to 1*s.* 6*d.*, 1*d.* from 2*s.* 6*d.* to 7*s.* 6*d.*, and 2*d.* from 10*s.* to 20*s.* There were ten denominations, which left some gaps. For example, anyone wishing to send 2*s.*, had to buy two 1*s.* orders, and there was then no method of sending odd pence by the addition of stamps. This was then changed in 1884, when fourteen denominations were introduced, the poundage revised in the customer's favour, and broken amounts might be made up with stamps. These advantages helped to build up a sale to 33 millions a year, and when, in 1903, the postal order purchase and cashing facilities were extended to almost every post office in the country the total again nearly trebled. At this time also all the colonies and dependencies of the British Empire were invited to join a scheme whereby British postal orders were available for remittances to and from the mother country and between one possession and another. The majority of the nations approached agreed to join the scheme.

The introduction of money orders and postal orders is closely allied to the other financial services conducted by the Post Office to-day—the Savings Bank, payment of State pensions, Family Allowances, Service Allowances, Savings Certificates, and so on. Their growth is in itself an interesting study. But, as in the case of the telegraph and telephone services, they are not sufficiently identified with the Posts to warrant description here.

15

HOW THE POST OFFICE
DEALS WITH CRIME

Two types of crime are directly concerned with the mails. The first is the obvious one of stealing letters and parcels during transit, and the second the use of the mails for the transmission of prohibited material. In the latter category there are the technical sins of people who insist on posting such things as snakes, dangerous acids, and inflammable products—such as matches and fireworks (they all appear in the Posts from time to time); and there are the more reprehensible matters forbidden because of indecency, prejudice to the security of the State, espionage, and so on.

As the writer has stressed, the sanctity of the mails has always been regarded as something more than the mere protection of valuables. Any robbery of postal packets during transit was, and often still is, punished with far greater severity than would be the case of stealing an article of similar value from a shop or house. The Post Office has from the earliest times shown itself peculiarly efficient in running mail-robbers to earth, as the following case from the early nineteenth century shows. It occurred on a night in January 1827, when the mail coach from Dover was on the way to the Post Office in Lombard Street. It was carrying a heavy load of mail from the principal European countries, each in a separate bag, and the entire load was enclosed in a heavy case.

The clerk who stood by as the porters unstrapped the case immediately noticed long knife cuts in the leather. The letter bill enclosed by the French postal authorities in Paris was still there, but a quick glance showed that the bag from Italy was missing. By the return coach that night, a Post Office investigator travelled to Dover, and by the same coach an urgent letter was sent to Calais asking for the immediate presence of the officials in charge of overseas mails in that town, and of the master of the French packet boat which had carried the mail across the Straits. As a matter of record, the presence of these gentlemen was found to be unnecessary, because at Dover the Customs showed that they had examined the mail and checked that all the bags tallied with the letter bill. The robbery had therefore taken place on the coach. There then followed some detection work by the Post Office official which would do credit to any member of the C.I.D. to-day. He covered every stage on the way to London, asking questions of ostlers, landlords, stable boys, and ticket agents. He soon found some promising clues.

Three men had been travelling outside the coach as passengers, booked to different stages and seemingly strangers to one another. They had all alighted at Canterbury, and subsequent investigation among people who were abroad that night proved that two of these passengers talked together out of sight of the coach guard. They were joined by a third, who subsequently went towards London by the coach. This at least seemed a suspicious coincidence, and the G.P.O. sleuth started enquiring at other inns in Canterbury. At the " Rose " he found a waiter who remembered two men ordering a post-chaise for London, at the same time asking for a private room where they could wait until the vehicle was ready. The waiter went to tell them that it was time to leave, and surprised them with a number of letters on the table, which they hurriedly tucked into their pockets. The post-chaise was traced all along the road to London until a night watchman was found who remembered two men alighting from such a vehicle by his box on the night in question.

The description of one of the men tallied with that of a well-known thief named Partridge. Eventually he was arrested and identified by numerous witnesses brought to London from the stages along the Dover Road. In the leisurely manner of those times, the trial did not come up—at Maidstone—for eight months. It seemed a foregone conclusion that Partridge would be found guilty, but he caused a sensation by providing irrefutable evidence that he had been in the West Country for most of January. He was acquitted.

There was a sequel long afterwards. The G.P.O. official who had made the investigations happened to be walking in the City when he saw Partridge walk into an inn in Bishopsgate. Just as he approached the door he gave a shout, and from an upper window a head appeared—another Partridge. The case was dead and buried so far as the police were concerned, but the Post Office wanted to know the real facts about the Dover Mail mystery. A well-known thief was invited to have an off-the-record chat. He came and explained the whole plot. Partridge had a brother barely a year older than himself. Few people knew of the brother's existence, because he had spent most of his life in America. But a fence saw the possibilities of a perfect alibi and arranged the whole scheme. The thief who revealed this also knew how the robbery had been carried out: the case had been slashed while lying in the coach office at Dover, where it had remained for four hours after the Customs inspection. By a strange twist to this strange case, the thief invited to explain the mystery was actually the second man of the conspiracy, a fact which he confessed later when on the scaffold for horse-stealing.

Mail robberies of this type are now a rarity, and there is a more profitable field for discussion in the manner in which the Post Office deals with the second category of " postal crime ". The prevention of the transmission of prohibited material is a delicate subject, for it necessarily touches on the sanctity of the mails. This sanctity is considered so important that it is an offence to open or intercept letters without an express warrant signed by a Secretary of State, although, of course, Post Office officials may open undeliverable letters in order to dispose of them. As mentioned elsewhere, they also have the power to open letters in the international service at the request of an officer of the Customs and Excise, but it should be emphasised that the Post Office has no independent power to open or tamper with correspondence. It is interesting to trace the history of the practice whereby correspondence has been opened for purposes of State.

The Tudor Posts started at a time when intrigue was rife. Apart from disaffected areas in England and the troubles across the

Border and the constant plotting of *émigrés* living in Europe, there was also the more open and still more dangerous menace of Spain. Those responsible for running the Posts in the sixteenth and seventeenth centuries were in something of a quandary. The provision of a national service for the use of the public able to afford the charges enabled a considerable amount of useful information to be gleaned by discreet examination of the mail, but it also made communication—and intrigue—much easier. On the other hand, suppression of the public's privilege of the use of the Posts merely fostered the growth of illegal systems where no examination was possible. Walsingham, the most astute of all Elizabeth's advisers, regularly tapped both general and diplomatic mails. It was done quickly and secretly, and often no action was taken on what was read, because Walsingham was glad to keep this useful source of information available for his Queen and himself.

Under the régime of Cromwell the letter-opening activities were naturally to the fore, and they were continued when Charles II came to the throne. There were many stories of a remarkable machine which was kept in the General Letter Office. The claims that it could open and seal letters so perfectly that the tampering defied detection are not particularly remarkable, but the boast that it could also take facsimile copies of letters certainly is. These stories are, however, well founded, and it is reported that Charles was so fascinated by the device that he used to go around at night to watch it work. It was destroyed when the Letter Office was burned down in the Great Fire of London, and with it the secret went too. Many chemists and photographers have debated the system which was used if contact copying was possible, as it seems to have been.

All this letter-opening was tacitly permitted, but in the Act of 1711 the practice was specifically mentioned, postal officials having to swear that they would not open letters except by written orders from the Secretaries of State or in order to deal with insufficiently and wrongly addressed packets. At this time many Jacobites were arrested on the strength of evidence obtained from their correspondence. The practice continued steadily during the eighteenth century, but it seems to have been restricted mainly to matters affecting the security of the State and to catch criminals. Apart from actual opening, letters were regularly "candled"—holding them before a flame—to see if they had an enclosure and should therefore be charged at double rates.

In 1844 matters came to a head. An M.P. presented a petition from a number of people claiming redress because their letters had been opened by the Post Office. The Home Secretary brusquely admitted that he had given the warrant for them to be opened, and he added that he had no intention of giving any explanation. Neither the public nor Parliament seem to have realised that the 1837 Act had continued the permission for letter-opening which had been contained in the 1711 legislation. The controversy which then arose centred around the letters of Mazzini (the Italian patriot living in London at the time) in particular, and the sanctity of the public's correspondence in general. There now started an agitation that swept the country with almost as much fervour as the campaign for the Penny Post six years earlier. The Press threw itself into the attack armed with criticism ranging from the sonorous periods of Macaulay down to crude cartoons. *Punch* was particularly active. One of the most popular cartoons appearing in that journal showed the Home Secretary reviewing the ranks of London's postmen on a military parade. Orders being given were:

" Present letters; feel for seal."
" Thumb on seal; open letters."
" Read letters; re-fold letters."
" Re-seal letters; pocket letters."

Quite the most bizarre turn of the whole campaign was the revelation that the letters of the M.P. who had presented the original petition had been subject to scrutiny because of his connection with the Chartists. With all this news, the anger of the House of Commons was aroused. It was possibly all very well that a foreigner living in England should have his letters opened because of the risk of his involving the country in European strife, but the elected representatives of the nation had no intention of acquiescing in an arrangement which made their own correspondence reading matter for the Government. Although the debates were among the most angry and protracted of that

Parliament, the strong majority which Peel enjoyed ensured the defeat of the motion for a Select Committee.

It is probably true to say that the Government learned its lesson, even though it would not give way. The law has never been changed, though quite often challenged. In the uneasy times of to-day, Parliament would probably agree that the permission is justified in special cases. The powers are certainly now used with great restraint under the Post Office Act of 1908.

No better proof of the justification of these powers to examine letters can be desired than their use in the case of a plot to murder the nation's Prime Minister, Mr. Lloyd George, just after the end of the first World War. An agent attached to Scotland Yard's Special Branch learned of the plan through an informer. A woman living in the Midlands was the instigator of the rumoured scheme. She was known as an extreme suffragette. She had a son-in-law who was a chemist at Southampton, and he was influenced by her to such an extent that he was ready to be a party to a diabolical scheme to kill the Premier with the South American poison, curare. It was to be shot into his leg on the barb of a dart while he was playing golf.

On the face of it, the report sounded like one of the more imaginative efforts of a thriller-writer. But orders were issued to the Post Office to check letters arriving at the suspects' houses in Southampton and the Midlands. To the surprise of the police, within twenty-four hours the Post Office was able to supply a photograph of a letter written by the woman which contained damning proof. Shortly afterwards a parcel postmarked " Southampton " and addressed to the woman was stopped. On orders from the Secretary of State, it was opened. It contained a bottle of liquid and a warning that if any of it touched a sore finger it would mean death. All the parties concerned were charged and given prison sentences. Here, at least, the carefully safeguarded authority to open letters had averted a tragedy which, at that time, would have changed history, for Mr. Lloyd George was engaged in the discussions on the Peace Treaty.

Anonymous letters containing violent abuse, unfounded charges, and often a mass of indecent phrases are a common phenomenon of the Posts in every country. Prominent people are accustomed to them, but persons whose names come into the limelight through Press reports for some reason or another are naturally bewildered and disgusted at the vicious and unreasoning tirades which are sent to them by cranks, and mild mental and psychological cases. An unsigned letter is not, of course, illegal in itself, but if it is obscene or libellous it certainly is.

Psychology plays an important part in tracking down these offending anonymous letter writers. G.P.O. investigators, working at the request of and in co-operation with the police, have from long experience in dealing with such cases worked out a routine of suspects. First is the person most gravely scandalised, then the person who indignantly reports the matter, and, thirdly, the person with the most to gain. It is a peculiar twist of the human brain that most poison-pen addicts write to themselves. The reason is two-fold: to divert suspicion and to bring notoriety. Their objectives are not reached if the victim keeps the charges to himself.

The tracking of the source of anonymous letters is a long and patient business. The nature of the offence indicates a repressed, cunning mentality in which the sentiments expressed under the believed safety of a message sent by mail are usually the very antithesis of the writer's normal social behaviour. The characterisation in the famous play, *Poison Pen*, perfectly portrayed the psychology of an anoymous letter writer, and, unless the person slips up in some way, a long and painstaking period of investigation is necessary to trace the writer.

Scientific aids for this purpose are numerous. The identity of the paper is, for instance, ascertainable. To avoid purchase of paper, some writers tear a sheet out of an old book or use a blank scrap of an old letter. It is an unwise move if they go too far back for their supply, for the constituents of paper are certain signposts to identity. Esparto grass was not used industrially until 1861, mechanical wood pulp came into use four years later, and chemical wood pulp in 1880. Under a microscope, the ingredients of these processes are easily identified. Esparto grass has long, thin fibres and a mass of stumpy little sections, and wood pulp has minute pieces of wood and blobs of fluff, different in mass according to mechanical or chemical processing. This examination is made after a piece of the paper has been boiled in a weak alkali solution, a drop of which is then placed on a slide and stained. Even when the type of paper has been identified in this way, its make can be still further classified according to the type of rag, grass, or wood; the chemical added for glazing and the dye for colouring. From this, manufacture can be checked, and then the shops supplied in the suspect's zone of operations. Eventually there may be a shop assistant who well recalls selling such stationery to one of the suspected persons.

Much of the scientific investigation work of this nature is carried on in a small building near the Law Courts, which is the Department of the Government Chemist, probably the oldest scientific crime-detection laboratory in the world. It was set up in 1842 primarily to detect adulteration in tobacco. Although most of its present work concerns major crime detection, checking of food purity standards, and so on, it also has research to perform on behalf of the Post Office. Savings Bank books are sent for detection of suspected alterations, and postage stamps believed to have been used twice have attention. It is surprising what trouble people will go to for the purposes of saving $2\frac{1}{2}d$. Nearly always traces of the erased cancellation can be found, and the resultant fine could pay for the average person's postage-stamp costs for life.

Identification of handwriting, disguised or otherwise, has long since passed beyond the stage of theories put forward by character-delineators. Photographic enlargements many times the original size are made: a series from the anonymous letter and another series from a specimen of the suspect's writing. The characteristics which it is impossible to delete except by writing backwards or upside down will be evident. Even in the exceptions the deceit will fail on the reversible letters such as o, w, and m, i, d and p, n and u. The slope, height of letters (which always decreases to the end of the line), angularity, roundness, thickness, and flourishes will provide many parallels. This method, by the way, provided damning similarities in the Lindberg baby kidnapping case when a specimen of Hauptmann's writing and the ransom note were compared.

Sometimes it is necessary to read a postmark which is illegible because the black is faint on the dark colour of the stamp. It is very simple to make a cancellation show up clearly by photographing it with a colour filter—the colour cutting out all the colour rays of the stamp, so that in the photograph only the cancellation mark appears. Another all-too-common postal crime concerns the attempts to send bets to bookmakers or submit football pool entries in envelopes which bear a postmark earlier than the actual time when the letter was used. It usually entails the use of an envelope posted by the criminal to himself and then in some way slipped into the betting office.

Fluorescence caused by ultra-violet rays is invaluable in the detection of the erasures. When photographed in ordinary light or examined under microscopes the paper may seem to have no details of erasure at all. Photographed under ultra-violet light, traces of the original writing may appear, and the stain of the eradicator will certainly be seen. There is no chemical ink-eradicator or bleacher known to-day which does not leave a mark visible under the fluorescent glow of ultra-violet light.

Pencil marks leave no trace identifiable by the ray methods. However, microscopic photography used on suspected pieces of paper will usually give the evidence required. If a soft rubber had been used there will be minute pieces of the rubber adhering to the paper. A harder rubber will show that the fibres of the paper have been distorted by the friction necessary to remove the markings. Sometimes, if a hard lead produced the original writing, the pencil strokes will have compressed the fibres, so that, covered with a film of grease and then soaked in a staining agent, the water will penetrate more slowly where the writing had been and a faint outline in white will appear after the surrounding paper has changed colour.

Although the constant worry of the Treasury when the first stamp designs were being considered was the possibility of forgery, there has only been one major case of the use of spurious postage stamps. It was unusual, because the criminal was never punished, though it is almost certain that his identity became known years afterwards.

He was a Post Office clerk, and his activities concerned the telegraphic service and not the mails. He started his nefarious operations shortly after the Post Office took over the telegraph service in 1870, being engaged to work in the Stock Exchange Telegraph Office, where, in the days before telephones, the large amount of business conducted may well be imagined. Twenty words could then be sent for a 1s., and naturally a 1s. postage stamp was then invariably used, even if stamps of smaller values were needed to make up the fee for words in excess of the minimum charge.

The Stock Exchange Office dealt with a considerable proportion of the 8 million telegrams sent during every year during the period the fraud is believed to have been carried on, and no doubt this particular clerk took care to work long and hard at the busiest window with commendable conscientiousness.

He devised as near perfect a system as it is possible to imagine. His forgeries were quite good, though there was no watermark, and he must have had some confederates for this side of the business. Armed with a stock of his home-made 1s. stamps, he used to sit down at his window ready for business. Brokers' messengers brought their telegrams, the clerk counted the words, named the fee, and passed the stamps to the customer for affixing to the form. This was then handed back for transmission. It will be noted that the stamp was in the possession of the purchaser for a few seconds only, and there was no reason for him to examine the stamp with any care.

The telegram was then ready for the usual routine. The clerk cancelled the stamp and passed the form to the wire-room. As soon as it was despatched, it was filed away and, after a reasonable wait for queries, sold as waste paper.

In 1872, by which time it was later estimated that he may have made £30,000 on the basis of 1,000 stamps a day, the forger retired on the grounds of ill health, with a pension into the bargain! He was able to enjoy the peace and security which is so rarely the lot of the criminal (who, unlike this gentleman, never know when it is advisable to stop), and not a breath of suspicion was aroused until 1898. A collector found a stamp on which the check letters were wrong, but the Post Office seems to have done little about an isolated instance, and another fourteen years passed by. Then, in 1912, a stamp-dealer bought scores of them and realised they were forgeries. They had come from bales of waste paper bought from the Post Office by a paper maker whose warehouse was at Watford. He had retired just after buying the waste (which he had contracted to destroy, incidentally) and simply left the material as it was. In 1912 workmen went to repair the roof of the warehouse, moved the bales out of the way, and one of them thought that he might be able to sell the stamps on the old forms which he saw scattered about. The information about the whereabouts of these sacks of stamped forms came to the Post Office in an anonymous letter, believed to have been written by one of the workmen, who quarrelled over the division of the money received from the sale of the first handful taken away. The Post Office hurried over to Watford and bought the waste back from the owner. Then the whole story was out.

Dishonesty will, of course, always find a loophole in any accounting system, but the arrangements in use in the 'seventies must have been lax indeed to allow thousands of telegrams to be sent without any balance against the number of 1s. stamps used. Even the daily discrepancy must have been large. We may be quite certain that no such scheme would work to-day.

The nineteenth-century stamp-forger did not attempt to copy the watermark. To-day there would be methods available to him, but they would be easily detected. Watermarks cannot be forged on stamps without eventual discovery. The suspected stamp is covered with a thin film of powder which has a fluorescing property. It is then soaked in water while watched under ultra-violet rays. As the powder soaks up the water it glows. By placing a genuine stamp side by side, the rate at which the powder absorbs water can be watched. The genuine watermark will resist the soaking, the imitation will not, and so the outline of the faked watermark does not shine for a time like an illuminated shape surrounded by illumination. In the cruder method of making watermarks, by outlining the mark in wax, the shining outline is much sharper, while the wax will itself glow in another colour.

In cases where it is suspected that letters or parcels have been opened *en route*, the ultra-violet ray will provide tell-tale evidence of tampering.   Different brands of sealing wax have different fluorescing colours, and a wax melted in a proper cup shines differently from one which has been melted in a match flame. Consequently, re-softening of the wax may show two colours from the same piece of wax or there may be a second blob on top from a different stick, which will again show itself.

The most intricate stamp forgeries are invariably on stamps which have a high value as collector's pieces.   Although such cases are not of direct connection with Post Office affairs, the methods of detection indicate what can be done should anyone be foolish enough to start a stamp forgery on a large scale.   In the case of a valuable Indian stamp — valuable because of an inverted frame in a few specimens issued a century ago—photographs taken under fluorescence indicated that two plates had been made from a normal specimen of the stamp, after which one was reversed for printing.   The plates were one-hundredth of an inch out of register, proving the forgery.

16

MAILS BY AIR

WITHIN a few months of Wilbur and Orville Wright achieving the first controlled flight in a power-driven aeroplane, many people were suggesting that the new invention, even if it could not carry heavy goods or passengers, would be ideal for carrying small quantities of urgent mail. The idea was a little more revolutionary than it might now seem, for the Wright Brothers believed that the aeroplane was purely of military use. One of the first experimental trips with mail made in this country took place at an air meeting in Blackpool in 1910. Grahame-White, the first man to fly an aircraft by night, took a mail bag for a seven-mile trip round Blackpool, landed, and then had them posted in the usual way. The letters were marked with the information that they had gone by air before starting on their land journey in the care of the Post Office and are now, as a matter of interest, of considerable value. To a generation always familiar with the aeroplane, this 1910 effort may appear a little pathetic, but it did serve to focus public attention on the possibility of aeroplanes carrying mails. The weather was bad, and the circular route was a last-minute substitution for a rather more ambitious idea: to fly the mails from Blackpool to Southport, which would have been better publicity, for the aeroplane would have crossed straight over the estuary of the Ribble and saved the land detour of some thirty-five miles.

The first Post Office-sponsored air mail service started in September 1911, between Hendon and Windsor. It was part of the celebrations of the Coronation of George V. Some 130,000 letters and postcards were carried (at the usual rate of 1d.) and each was postmarked " First United Kingdom Aerial Post ".

The mail bag hatch on a Europe-bound air liner.

Helicopter Air Mail service

The World War of 1914, which was to develop the aeroplane out of all recognition, did, of course, at the same time defer any further air mail experiments, though plenty of military documents passed on the air ferry services between London and Paris and Dover and Etaples, and it is worthy of note that the official details of the signing of the Armistice came from Paris to London in a De Havilland machine.

In 1919, civil aviation developed rapidly. On 1 May civil air services had been authorised, and three companies were running regular services from London to Paris, the trip taking between two and a half and three hours. Operating cost was heavy, dependence on good weather made the service unreliable, and from a commercial point of view of profitable operation these pioneer passenger flights were a failure, though as a postal service they were promising.

It is worth while contrasting the British attitude to commercial flying with that in America at this time. In the United States nearly all scheduled air routes were operated by the U.S. Post Office, a system which lasted until 1926, when mail contracts were given to private concerns, and the securing of them made all the difference between success and failure. The huge distances of America, with large towns in every part of the country, did, of course, make internal air mail services an entirely different proposition from the organisation of internal and foreign services in Britain. However, it was soon seen that British air lines needed subsidising just as the first passenger steamships had been helped nearly a century earlier. This became very evident to the Government in the winter of 1920-1, when the air service on the London-Paris routes was reduced to one flight a day, and the Holland route abandoned temporarily. In March, 1921, a subsidy was granted based on receipts.

The full-scale development of regular air mail services came with the formation of Imperial Airways on 1 April 1924. This organisation operated regular schedules to Paris, Brussels, Cologne, Amsterdam, Hanover, Berlin, Basle, and Zurich. Not until 1929 was the first long-distance service from London to India put into operation. Difficulties with the Persian Government prevented the operation of the Basra-Karachi section, though the stage as far

as Basra ran regularly, carrying 340 lb. of mail on each weekly
trip. The route through to India was flown in 1930 on a round-
about itinerary over Europe because of further diplomatic difficulties, this time with Italy.

It was in 1934 that the Government stated, through the Under-
Secretary of State for Air, that it was the aim to carry all first-
class (overseas) mail matter by air without surcharge, and this
ambition was gradually turned into reality.　In March, 1936,
arrangements were made for first-class mail for Scandinavia to be
carried by air without surcharge, and this was gradually extended
to most of Europe. After considerable discussion in Parliament on
civil air services generally, the Empire Air Mail scheme was
planned for inauguration in 1937. Under this far-seeing and boldly
conceived service all first-class mail (letters and postcards) between
Britain and the nations of the Commonwealth served either by
Imperial Airways or the air services running in Australia, India,
and South Africa, were to go by air.　The exception was, of
course, Canada, through the barrier of the Atlantic.

The services were to provide a comprehensive coverage at
frequent intervals. Nine flights a week were scheduled for Egypt;
five to India, three to Malaya and Australia, and two to South
Africa. Apart from two land-plane services to India, the main
routes were to be covered by flying boats.　Forty new aircraft
were ordered to build the Imperial Airways fleet up to a total of
seventy-six machines.

In 1936, the year before this scheme came into operation,
Imperial Airways machines flew $4\frac{3}{4}$ million aircraft miles. As the
scheme got under way—and it was slower than had been hoped—
the mileage increased enormously. When the final route of the
scheme was inaugurated with the flight of a flying boat loaded with
mail for Australia on 28 July 1938, the average weight of letters
despatched from Britain reached 19 tons in a week, and in that
year the machines flew nearly 9 million aircraft miles.

Payment to Imperial Airways for carrying mail over the Imperial
routes was at a contract rate of £900,000 per annum.　The
contract also provided for a subsidy payment averaging £600.000
per annum. Elsewhere, the Post Office paid heavily for the use

of foreign air services. For mail to South America, for instance, the bill in 1937 came to £100,000—the money going to German and French aviation companies.

In the same year the inland air services rapidly developed their mail-carrying arrangements. There were 5,300 miles of routes over and around the British Isles, and many regular services carried mails. The Post Office had come to regard the aeroplane as another form of mail transport, to be used when it provided advantages of speed over rail and road.

To-day the air mail services are such a normal feature of the British postal arrangements that the carriage of a large proportion of letters by air is of no surprise to the general public, if they think about the matter at all. But in the islands off Britain the coming of the regular air mail is a boon that only the people living in those isolated areas can really appreciate. To Northern Ireland, the Scottish isles, and the Channel Islands the inland air mail services have speeded up deliveries enormously. Despite the severity of the storms in winter in such areas as the Orkneys and the Hebrides, failure of a schedule is very rare indeed. The writer vividly recalls days towards the end of the war when R.A.F. flights were suspended through bad weather, yet on the radar plotting screens the echoes of the passenger mail planes were still seen flying steadily on their familiar routes, hugging the coast to avoid mountains invisible in the drifting sleet and low clouds.

For some of these lonely places a letter which used to take four days to reach Glasgow is now delivered on the same day as it is posted. The machines are flying in one of the most unpredictable climates in the world and over what airmen call "thorny ground". It is aeroplanes like these that are responsible for the carriage of a large proportion of the 69½ million letters which went by air on the inland air services in 1948-9.

In that year, too, the overseas mail totals took a leap upwards. No fewer than 129 million items were sent by air, a 30 per cent. increase over the previous year being largely due to the intro-duction in July 1948 of an "all up" service to the greater part of Europe, whereby all first-class mail went without extra charge by air unless there was no service which would beat the ship and

8

railways deliveries.   At the same time the lightweight 6*d.* air letters service was made available to all countries of the world outside Europe.

The final chapter of air mail development is certainly not yet written, even though it is now possible to send a letter anywhere in the world by air. Experiments have been made with collecting and delivering mail bags by helicopter during the hours of darkness. For areas badly served by main line railways and necessitating long road journeys for the motor vans, the helicopter may provide a solution for quick service from a central post office. It may well be that in a year or two the hovering postman will be as normal a feature of isolated villages as the red van and the telephone box outside the general shop is to-day.

The final comment on the importance of the air mail to-day may well be left to figures of its cost. In 1948-9 conveyance of mails by British aircraft operators cost £3,951,208.   This was more than twice the cost of the mails that went by sea, and over half the cost of mails sent by rail. Truly we have advanced a long way from those days of the sixteenth century when Sir Brian Tuke paid out 12*d.* per day for a Post horse.

17

CONTRABAND MAIL

I N the economic fortress that is Britain to-day a great burden of responsibility has been thrown on the Post Office in connection with Customs checks on the outgoing and the incoming mails. Virtually everything is subject to duty or purchase tax, and prohibition of, or licence for, permission to import when coming into the country, and there is a long list of goods which must not be sent out of the country except by licence.

Consequently, the control of foreign letters and parcels in both directions is an onerous and expensive task which absorbs man-power and time alike. Not a little of the trouble with the out-going mails comes from the persistence of the public in failing to enquire about regulations, and a steady stream of packets make their way back to the senders, adding considerably to the work of both the postal and Customs authorities.

Letters present similar problems. The tolerance about foreign mail inspection has had to be restrained because of the practice of people sending Treasury notes, stamps, and documents of value overseas in an effort to outwit the currency restrictions. Even with the existence of this practice, the examination of letters for exchange control purposes is confined to ensuring that they contain no illicit enclosures, and there is no question of censorship. But the deliberate contravention of the regulations has made routine examination needful, though it seems obvious that without the employment of enormous staffs the authorities must rely largely on sample checks.

Rightly, no information of the methods used to see that cor-respondents do not outwit the law is forthcoming, but some idea of the size of the job can be gleaned from the fact that in 1948-9 the Post Office commercial accounts state that £761,094 were collected in Customs duties on parcels. The London Foreign Parcels Section is at the Royal Agricultural Hall, Islington, where many of the 14 million incoming and 8 million outgoing parcels are handled. It is the duty of the Post Office to open the parcels, submit them for Customs examination, and close them again. As anyone receiving parcels from abroad will know, not every packet is opened, although all are liable to be dealt with for Customs examination. The officials get to know which parcels are perfectly reliable and contain only the articles listed on the outside. Typical are the parcels of foodstuffs sold in America and elsewhere which are all ready wrapped for the purchaser and despatched by the supplying firm. Each mail delivery from the United States and the Dominions will contain hundreds of such parcels, all identical in appearance, and, clearly, it would be following the letter rather than the spirit of the regulations to open each one.

There are the cases of deliberate attempts to smuggle to be considered. Many optimists—they can hardly be classed with the professional smugglers—try to send tobacco and cigarettes through the Post. Often they address the parcels to themselves while they are abroad. Such parcels are very easily detected by shape, weight, or smell, and no doubt the tobacco and cigarettes seized to a weight of 19,857 lb. in 1948-9 came partly from postal contraband. It may be of slight comfort to the perpetrators to know that they went to the Services comforts committees and criminal lunatic asylums for solacing the recipients in the accustomed way, and to the Royal Botanic Gardens at Kew, where doubtless the "noisome weed" has since decimated the blight on valuable hot-house plants.

It is curious to mark the blind faith that some people have in the security of a misleading description of the contents of a parcel. Scores who write "confectionery" on the outside of a parcel containing a box of cigarettes, or " tinned fruit " on a cylindrical packet full of perfume, indignantly wonder why their idea failed to deceive the cynics of the Customs and Excise services. They should remember that X-ray machines can look through parcels very easily and see what is really inside them before it is decided that they should be opened. Also, the authorities know exactly what a given area of paper, string, and a can of peaches weigh, or what the ratio of weight to volume is for sweets as compared with cigarettes. The instruments which they can use are referred to in Chapter 15. The part they play is referred to in a significant item tucked away in the Appropriation Accounts of the Customs and Excise for 1948-9: " Instruments and materials for revenue purposes: £9,645 13s. 9d."

The authorities can, of course, call in experts to help them. A typical case occurred towards the end of 1949, when a number of parcels was opened in routine Customs examination at the London Postal Depot. Ostensibly containing nuts and rice, some included pearls as well. Enquiries were made by Customs officers at the London premises of the merchant to whom the parcels were addressed, and there some letters in an unknown language were found. These, of course, had come through the mails without being examined.

As it seemed possible that the letters had some bearing on the smuggling and might indicate a premeditated arrangement to pass pearls in bags of foodstuff, experts were invited to attempt their translation. Mr. G. Meredith-Owens, a temporary assistant in the Oriental Books Section of the British Museum identified the characters as an unusual Hebrew script and the language as Persian, with a little Hebrew. A vital sentence read: " The nuts are inclined to be yellowish, so their lustre is not very good."

" Lustre" clearly referred to pearls and not to nuts, and the inevitable end came with prosecution and a fine of £1,500. The case shows why the Posts are not used for any large-scale professional smuggling. Should suspicion be aroused, the addressee for certain, and the sender in all probability, will be unaware that their trick has been discovered until too late.

An unusual form of postal smuggling which has constantly to be watched is the sending of indecent or obscene material from abroad and, to a lesser extent, through the inland mails. Importation of such material is prohibited under the Customs laws, and the decision as to what constitutes an infringement rests on the authorities. Contrary to popular belief, there is no "secret list " of such articles, nor is it necessary to base a ruling on a previous court case, for obviously many such articles may be arriving for the first time. Like most of this country's laws where a degree of tolerance is allowed on action, the matter is dealt with on a basis of common sense, which finds few critics.

18

THE POST OFFICE IN
TIME OF WAR

THE Posts had first been organised to cope with the courier
services of a fifteenth century war between England and
Scotland. In century after century they were called on to provide
a similarly vital service for the prosecution of hostilities.
Probably the first major postal service for an army overseas was
that organised in connection with Marlborough's campaigns.
Nothing is known about the facilities for the ordinary soldier to
enable him to write home, but the intricate routes set up to keep
the Government in touch with the headquarters was certainly used
for the private correspondence of Marlborough himself. Letters
to his wife are still preserved. They went through the field posts.

In the Napoleonic Wars, too, the Post Office was in the field
with the armies. This time its system was definitely available for
the troops of the line. But it was not until the war in the Crimea
broke out that the Post Office had to face the problem of handling
large quantities of mail to and from a large army able and anxious
to correspond with their families. The tradition, as it now is, that
troops on active service get special privileges on the cost of posting
letters began at this time, and the gunner at Inkerman could write
about his adventures to his wife in England and post it home for
1*d*. So large did the quantities of mail become that French ships
were asked to help our own severely taxed transports, and the Post
Office set up a distributing organisation on the shores of the Black
Sea—the first Army post office in history. In the war of 1882
against Egypt and the Boer War the same organisation was set
up. After the end of the Boer War the experiences in that difficult campaign of maintaining touch with the widely scattered

forces were studied, and resulted in the formation of a Royal Engineers Postal Section in 1902. Staffed entirely by Post Office employees, it obtained practical experience during manœuvres, and in August 1914 it was ready to go into operation with a strength of ten officers and 290 other ranks. By the Armistice it had swollen to 4,000. It was then handling 12 million letters a week.

This force in the field did not, of course, include the staff at home which handled the mail for the troops. The sorting centre started work in a temporary building in Regent's Park, and as the menace of Zeppelin raids developed it was decentralised to various provincial towns. The mail went vast distances to reach its destination in many cases. The men in the Dardanelles campaign, for example, received letters which had been sent by merchant ship to Alexandria, then by any naval or supply vessel going to Mudros, and finally by minesweeper to the beaches of Gallipoli. This effort was beaten in the Second World War with the mail for Malta. Sometimes it had to go round the Cape, then up through the Red Sea and the Suez Canal to Alexandria. From there it went by submarine to the George Cross Island, packed in the vessel along with bags of flour, crates of children's shoes, and stacks of anti-aircraft shells, which was typical of the strangest cargoes ever carried in a ship of the Royal Navy.

In the Second World War both the difficulties of maintaining the mail service and the number of items to be handled were far greater than those of the First World War. From the outset, during the period of the so-called "phoney war" from September 1939 to May 1940, the whole peacetime basis disappeared. Decentralisation ordered by the Government compelled reorganisation of the national executive and control arrangements; the black-out made a task which has always reached its peak during the hours of night still more formidable; and the evacuation of children, mobilisation of menfolk for the armed services or war factories, and the movement of firms to the countryside sent the mail figures soaring.

Even though enemy raids fortunately did not aggravate the position in the first few months, the staff problem was immediately serious. Fifteen per cent. of the staff were in the Forces before the middle of September 1939. Painting over of the large glass

ᴏᴘ: An old print showing the interior of the travelling Post Office van on the ᴏndon and Birmingham railway in **1838**. Bᴏᴛᴛᴏᴍ: Interior scene on the travelling ᴏst Office on the London-Norwich run, British Railways. This picture was taken on the first trip after the **1939-45** war.

A modern Post Office railway sorting coach.

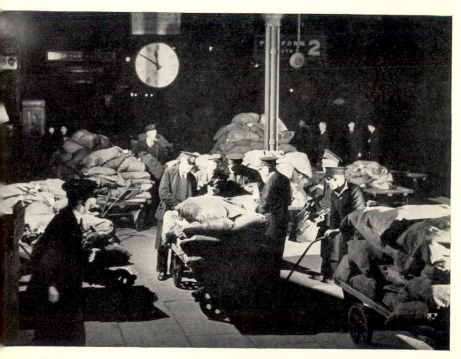

Top: Fixing the pouches for the Mail Train. Bottom: Night scene at Crewe station.

Just a day's work in the primary parcel sorting section at Mount Pleasant.

Post Office tube train arriving at Paddington station.

The Post Office carries on in wartime—one of the mobile offices set up in a heavily bombed area of London.

roofs of many sorting offices made the use of artificial light perpetual, making work even more difficult for the many new hands that came to fill the gaps. Then, after the bitter winter of 1939-40 came the raids of Britain's Finest Hour. Although some 73,000 men and women had joined the services, their older colleagues and the people who filled the gap nobly maintained the tradition of the Royal Mail. By mere statistics, the story is that over 700 decorations were conferred on Post Office workers of all grades, and 413 gave their lives. A few cases of the way the Post Office continued to operate in the face of every form of attack that the enemy could devise are contained in the official record of those years, Ian Hay's *The Post Office Went to War*.

London offices have the most stories to tell. In September 1940 twenty-three post offices were hit. In the great fire blitz of the following December the building in Wood Street housing three telephone exchanges and the essential parts of two others was hit several times, many of the staff remaining at their posts in the smoke and heat until the police and Fire Service officials ordered them out. The same night the Central Telegraph Office was gutted. In June 1943 the great sorting centre at Mount Pleasant received the most serious damage of its nine " incidents ": the parcels section was completely gutted.

In the infamous Coventry raid of November 1940, the head Post Office and sorting office were hit by incendiary bombs, but the fires were put out and all services continued. Post Office premises at Birmingham, Bristol, Southampton, and Plymouth suffered in subsequent raids, though because of instant repair work the public outside the vicinity would never have known about it. The raids were exacting their toll and bringing their stories of heroism. There was the postman-driver mortally wounded by a shell splinter as he made the last collection at the village of Blackpill, between Swansea and Mumbles. There were only a few letters in the mail bag which he clutched as he lay beside the pillar box he had been emptying. Not until full arrangements were in hand for its conveyance to the sorting office would he consent to be moved to hospital, where he died a few hours later. Then there was the widow who ran a sub-post office at Cobholm Island, Great Yarmouth. Her tiny premises were seriously damaged in the night raid on the town. At 3 a.m. she knocked on a neighbour's house and asked permission to transfer her books and official material to a living-room. At 9 a.m. the following morning she opened for business. It was the day for paying out old age pensioners. She did not intend to fail them.

Dover postal services were naturally subject to uniquely heavy attack in their position within sight of the enemy coastline. At the time of Dunkirk the staff worked day and night to get away tens of thousands of telegrams handed in by the gaunt remnant of the B.E.F. Girl teleprinter operators had to be lifted away from their machines when physical exhaustion eventually overcame will power. During the years that followed Dover Post Office was bombed, shelled, and machine-gunned. One shell scored a direct hit on the telephone exchange, killing three operators. An emergency switchboard was operating two hours later.

A great service of the Post Office during the war, though it does not come within the province of this book, was the network of communications for the defence of the country. The size of it eventually exceeded that of the entire peacetime network. Even with this work allied to the essential service of keeping the public communications running, the employees were still ready to do more. Some 50,000 joined the Home Guard.

When the raids started the Post Office achieved miracles of extempore organisation, keeping the system of letter-distribution flexible enough to work without hindrance, even though sorting offices, railway stations, and other transport facilities were put out of action. The postman was always well on the scene at times of obstinate determination to keep life going or when he could relieve poignant moments with the good tidings he could carry. When the *Arundel Castle* arrived with sick and wounded prisoners repatriated from Germany, the first man to go on board the vessel was a Post Office official, to collect postcards and telegrams from the men. Special arrangements were made to rush these messages to their families.

It was a tragic yet courageous sight to see a blitzed street on an early morning during the air raid years: piles of rubble, the writhing lines of fire hoses—and the postman or postwoman moving through it all, delivering the mail to those houses which still stood. In areas where post offices were destroyed or damaged, or many people were evacuated into rest centres because of the destruction of their homes or the presence of delayed-action bombs, mobile post offices were put into operation. Originally these vehicles were built to serve large agricultural shows or sports meetings. Equipped with telephone, telegraph, and the usual postal facilities, they were planned as part of the campaign to stimulate Post Office business in the nineteen-thirties. The two pioneer trailers (which had the registration numbers GPO1 and GPO2) were rapidly augmented. They contributed something to that maintenance of morale which impressed the free world and infuriated Hitler, and the Government were fully alive to the importance of keeping the postal services going, whatever else suffered.

It is true to say that the millions of British men and women in uniform never seriously grumbled about anything except about the time taken for their mail to arrive. Commanding officers in the Burmese jungles, deep in the North African desert, and on lonely islands around the British coasts were continually reporting " morale is high, and will remain so, so long as the mail keeps coming through ". That there were complaints may be understood, even if they were unjustified. Mobile warfare from the Pacific to the Arctic Circle, with men sent without warning a thousand miles in a day, made the maintenance of the Army Posts a Herculean task. But the troops got their mail with uncanny speed, whatever they may have thought. The author recalls, while on attachment to the 9th United States Air Force, the delivery of mail posted in the New York area on one afternoon being delivered at an Air Force station in Hampshire twenty-two hours later. That was a bouquet for the U.S. Army Post Office, but quite as good is the story of an R.A.F. ground gunner whose wife posted him a parcel of laundered clothes on 4 June 1944 from her home in London. It was addressed to an Army Post Office number " somewhere in England ". On the night of 5 June the airman embarked in Poole Harbour for the Normandy beachhead. His parcel was delivered to him as he crouched in a trench behind Arromanches on the evening of 7 June—D-Day plus 1.

Nineteen forty-four was a peak year for Army postal activity. In the spring millions of troops of many nations were packed into Southern England; in the summer the majority of them had to be serviced in France. Simultaneously, other units were moving from Africa to Italy and Southern France, and still more were deploying all over the Far East. Compared with this the intricate system arranged for mail for prisoners of war on both sides was almost child's play.

The Army Post Office dealing with mails for British overseas forces was at Nottingham. It had aerodromes close at hand, was strangely unharmed by air raids, and serviced by a good railway system to all parts of the country. In the early part of 1944 a daily special train took the mails to the millions of men encamped on and around Salisbury Plain. A few weeks after D-Day this train was diverted to Tilbury or Dover. It is to the credit of the authorities that even at the worst times no restrictions were put on parcels for the Forces—those packets of duty-free cigarettes and of comforts from home which were so welcome. Innumerable trains were run specially to carry them. By the end of 1944 more than 600,000 packets a week were going to the Forces overseas. At this time, too, parcels were coming home in large quantities. Special trains were again needed to handle the Christmas parcels sent by troops, mainly on the duty-free concessions vouchers. They went to Bournemouth for Customs examination. There were other special Army postal centres. Canadian Forces' mail was sorted at Manchester in the early years of the war, and later at Addison Road, Kensington. In July 1942 the U.S. Army were given a central sorting depot at Sutton Park, near Walsall. In just over two years 1,200 special trains were run solely for the purpose of the U.S. Army mail.

The vast job of keeping the Forces in touch with their families could never have been achieved with the speed and ease that it was but for one thing: the innovation of airgraph letters. Under this system letters written on a special form were photographed on micro-film and then enlarged on receipt in this country. In this manner even the severely restricted accommodation of transport aircraft flying to outlying theatres of war could be used for mail carrying—many thousands of letters finding an odd corner among war stores and adding virtually nothing to the weight or volume of the main load.

19

TO-DAY AND TO-MORROW

To-day about one-third of the total non-industrial staff in the Civil Service is employed in the Post Office. The salaries, wages, and allowances of those engaged on the postal services absorb £60¾ millions a year. Conveyance of mail by contractors (excluding payment to overseas administrations) brings a bill of about £13½ millions, with £7 millions for the rail services, £700,000 for road transport, £1½ millions for maritime services, and £4 millions for air transport. In 1948 an average of 286 tons of air mail was carried every month, 93 tons on the internal services and 193 tons by overseas services. In 1949 the total had increased to 367 tons a month—113 tons inland and 254 tons overseas.

The gross sales of postage stamps by Postmasters reach an annual value of more than £71½ millions and the cost of their manufacture and supply (with postal orders) is about £347,000.

Motor vehicles, their supplies and maintenance, take £2¾ millions, postal apparatus such as mail bags, pillar boxes, sorting machinery, trolleys, and so on, absorbing over £1¼ millions, and uniforms and miscellaneous stores another £1¼ millions.

These statistics, based on the returns for 1948-9, are given in round figures because it is suggested that the general picture of the Post Office business of to-day can better be appreciated in that way. Now that conditions have returned to something approaching normal, these figures will doubtless serve as a rough basis for the general picture for some time. Even with changes, such as the increased parcels and foreign letter rate of the autumn of 1950, the additional staff needed to handle the later collections, further expansion of the air mail services, and an increase in wages which would seem inevitable at the time of writing will tend to balance somewhere on the basis shown in the figures above.

On the postal services alone the surplus in 1948-9 was £11 millions. This is really a " paper profit ", for the Post Office renders services without actual payment. The cost of work performed in connection with certain pensions and allowances and National Debt services is not recovered in cash by the Post Office.

Here lies the main problem of the Post Office to-day. Throughout its life the Post Office has had to fight the attitude of the central Government that it is partly—even primarily—a tax-gathering organisation. Sometimes it has been under the direction of Postmasters-General who have fought a losing battle against this attitude; often it has been in the control of officials who were very ready to acquiesce in this attitude because the office of Postmaster-General was a stepping-stone to still further advancement in a political career. It is, of course, right that the head of the postal services should be answerable to the nation and that he should be in the House of Commons or the Lords so that his every action can be examined in public. We have seen only too forcibly in recent years the difficulty of extracting information about nationalised industries where the head of the board or authority concerned can successfully hide behind the minister of the department most closely related to the particular industry or service. Probably the Posts concern every individual in Britain far more than coal, electricity, gas, transport, and so on, and it is a very precious privilege, not to be lightly given up, that anyone who fails to receive a letter at the time he thinks it should have dropped through his letter box can ask his M.P. to question the head of the organisation about it. He certainly cannot hope for such satisfaction if he has a query on his electric light bill or is angry about the dirt in the household coal. Similarly, for over one third of a million of Post Office employees alleged injustices can be righted when there is the likelihood of a " question in the House " to be answered.

There remains the problem of the deterioration in the Post Office services which must be admitted. Probably the golden age of our Posts followed the concessions of the Diamond Jubilee of 1897. It lasted until 1914. In those seventeen years the service was something that even an idealist like Rowland Hill would have considered as near perfect as anything can be. The very dates probably give us part of the answer as to what has since gone wrong. The service which was the very envy of the world was developed during a long period of peace and prosperity. Although social services increased the national expenditure towards the closing years, taxation was not the ruthless squeezing of every penny from every possible source that it became with major wars to finance. The profits of the postal services could be ploughed back in order to reduce costs and increase facilities.

Clearly a perfect balance sheet of a service devoted solely to the public good would show no profit. A Postmaster-General who offered to Parliament an account with a surplus would be as liable to censure as one who had to admit a loss. But that ideal (and it is surely no fault of the men in control at St. Martin's-le-Grand) is now a nebulous Utopian theory. Successive Chancellors of the Exchequer have taken the attitude of ordering increased charges based on what the market will stand. In the years between the wars there was agitation for a return of the Penny Post. To-day there is just as strong a demand for the return to the 1½d. rate. The latter seems as doomed to failure as the former. The Post Office is a revenue department as well as a public service.

The burdens which the Post Office carries for every other Government department also need examination. On a strictly cash basis, Post Office expenditure exceeded revenue by £6½ millions in 1948-9 on all services. This figure, of course, covers other branches, such as telephones and telegraphs. This position arises from services rendered to other Government departments for which no money is paid.

It has already been suggested that during the Second World War the abolition of invoices between one department and another was a sensible idea. The Post Office was on national service, providing a gigantic network of telephone and teleprinter lines for the armed services, carrying official and troops' mail without charge, and so on. It scarcely provides a reason to continue with such an arrangement in peacetime in order to show that postal charges cannot be reduced.

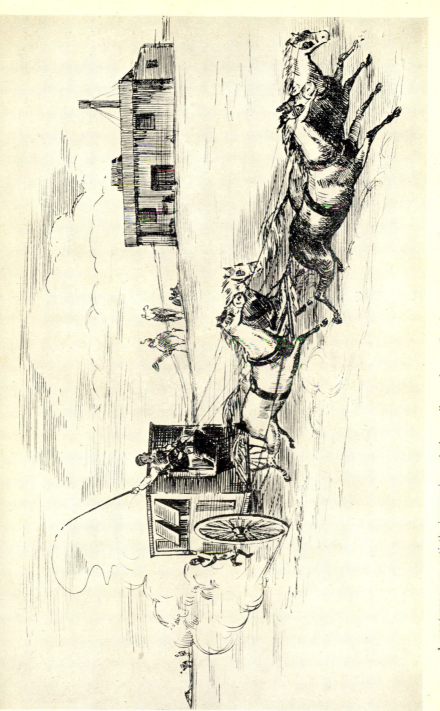

A contemporary artist's impression of the mail coach on the desert stage of the overland mail route to India.

The P and O "Hindostan" leaving Southampton on 24 September 1842, on the first run of the Indian mail service. The

An old print showing the Cunard Royal Mail steamship " Britannia " leaving Boston on 3 February 1844. A channel seven miles long was cut through the ice to enable the vessel to sail.

The 699 tons "Chusan", with an engine of 80 h.p., was the first P. and O. mail steamer to Australia.   She left Southampton

Yet economists believe that the present system is the lesser of all the possible evils. Of all Government departments, the Post Office is easily the most efficient in its relations with the public. Very few people are beyond walking distance of a post office. The postman visits all of them in their homes. If the hundreds of thousands of counter clerks and postmen kept strictly to their job of dealing with the public's letters, who would take over the other part of their present job? It has been said with some cynicism and much truth that the only licence that cannot be bought over a post office counter is a marriage licence. The postage stamp has become almost a sideline in the Post Office. Money orders, postal orders, insurance stamps, pensions, child allowances, licences for radio sets, motor cars, dogs, guns, and half a dozen other things are sold after forms have been completed. The Post Office is a bank, an information bureau, a dispenser of tobacco tokens, an almoner, a tax-collecting office, a recruiting bureau. It is almost certain that any queue in a post office is not held up because of slowness in issuing postage stamps.

Since 1938 the Post Office has become a great disseminator of official news and orders along with the B.B.C. (another child of the G.P.O.). Since the first A.R.P. and National Service booklet went to every home in the country, the postman has had to deal with a whole series of these mountains of literature. That it is the obvious medium by which to ensure that everyone knows the Government's plans on anything from national insurance to protection during atomic warfare does not preclude the basic unfairness that the Post Office should have to make ends meet while carrying out these and other services.

The alternative would be to use the other central and local government offices which exist. Food offices, police stations, employment exchanges, and National Insurance offices are admittedly widespread, but certainly not to the extent of the post offices. If they had to deal with all their own affairs instead of getting the Post Office to handle many of them, there would be an immediate increase in the size of the already swollen Civil Service, and, assuming that some of the burden would fall on the local authority in the provision of premises, an increase in the local rates. It is very probable that, too late, the public would

9

wish that the Post Office had carried on with its ancillary duties even if postage rates remained high.

Six people now do the work of every five on the postal services of pre-war years. Although the decrease in output may be partly due to shorter hours, which apply to postal officials just as they do in other industries (the general decrease in the nation's working week since 1938 has been from 46.5 hours to 45.3 hours), it is much more occasioned by the fact that the counter clerks are snowed under with work for which the Post Office is paid only by paper credits.

We can, in short, expect a return to a service comparable to the between-the-wars years, but its cost, like everything else, will be heavier.

20

THE DEVELOPMENT OF
THE POSTAGE STAMP

IN days gone by a stamp was a postmark; when the " small slip
of paper with a glutinous wash " was proposed by Rowland
Hill it was described as an adhesive label, and took the place
of the postmark as evidence of payment. Consequently, we must
go back many years before the arrival of the 1*d*. adhesive stamp
for the complete history of payment tokens on letters.

The first marks were those which came into use during Henry
Bishop's time in the middle of the seventeenth century. They
were rather crudely drawn circles, divided horizontally. In one
half was the day-date, in the other the first two letters of the
month. The earliest examples of letters bearing the Bishop mark
in the Public Record Office are dated 19 April (of the year 1661).
Nor were these marks used only for date checks. Bishop, despite
the fact that he lost the job of Postmaster-General as a result of
various charges against him of inefficiency, seems to have had a
business-like mind, and he was the real inventor of the postmark
slogan so common to-day. By the summer of 1661 he was
stamping announcements on letters which read: " Send answer by
the post at the Round House in Love Lane near Billingsgate "
and " The Post for all Kent goes every night from the Round
House, Love Lane, and comes every morning ".

Long after Bishop had died (and was buried, as the Henfield,
Sussex, parish records show in " Woolen only 1692 Mar 23 "),
his postmarks continued to be used. They were common for at
least a century after he started them.

Meantime Dockwra's Penny Post had started in London. This,
in the words of a contemporary writer, used " stamps to mark the

hour of the Day on all letters when sent out from their Office to be delivered, by which all persons are to expect their letters within one hour, (little more or less, from the time marked thereon, excepting such Letters as are to be conveyed to the Out-towns, and Remotest Parts, which will be longer) by which the cause of delay of Letters may easily be discern'd, viz. whether it be really in the Office, or their own Servants (or others) with whom Letters are left ".

Letters which Dockwra's postmen carried bore two stamps. One triangular one read " Penny Post Paid ", with the initial of the posting office in the centre; the other gave the time it should be delivered, such as " Mor 11 " or "Af 3 ". When the Post Office suppressed the Dockwra scheme and then started a palpable imitation of it they also adopted his postmarks. The difference was that official spelling left something to be desired—the triangle bore the words " Peny Post Payd "! Another notable change was the use of a circle instead of a heart shape for the time and day stamp. This brought the postmark into line with the Bishop mark used on provincial letters passing through the main road systems of the Post Office.

The next great development in postmarks was made by Ralph Allen, pioneer of the cross-Posts. As he had to pay his officials according to the number of letters they received for despatch, some sort of accountancy check had to be made at the head offices. For this purpose he instructed postmasters (and postmistresses, of which there were many by this time) to stamp all letters they handled. It was evidently left to the person concerned to procure his own stamp, and specimens which still exist show a variety of designs, most of them crude, but some of the more ingenious or artistic produced charming little designs, such as that of Bristol, which was a large B with " ris " in the upper loop and " tol " in the lower. As these Allen marks were merely for checking routes, no dates or other details appeared.

Towards the end of the eighteenth century there were various other changes in the design of postmarks which are of interest to the philatelist more than the student of postal history. An exception is the mileage postmark already noted in Chapter 8. It was in use by 1784, but, owing to disputes about the accuracy of the distances used, this device was abandoned twelve years later until new mileages were worked out. The revised marks are interesting because many are very similar to those in use to-day, particularly the marks in Ireland. They were circular, gave the name of the town round the edge and the date in the centre. The mileage appeared where the time is printed to-day.

We now come to the postmarks and stamps of the Penny Post of 1840. The stamps were not ready until four months after the scheme started, and for the interim postmarks had to be used. Hundreds of designs were adopted, once again the local postmaster presumably being left to procure his own. Most consisted of the figure " 1 " (denoting that 1*d*. had been paid) and some included the town of origin. They were usually stamped in red, but there are examples in black, magenta, purple, and blue. All this time the Treasury and Post Office were busily preparing for the first issue of stamps. It is regrettable that they did not have them ready when the Penny Post started, for the officials had been debating the matter for a long time.

Small pieces of paper to indicate payment of a fee were not a new idea. They were even used for postal purposes in Paris as far back as 1653, when, for a sou, a Parisian correspondent could buy a slip bearing the words " Port Payé " and have the letter delivered anywhere in the French capital. In Britain, slips of paper were affixed by seals on documents to indicate payment of tax, and they were also used for evidence of tax payment on patent medicines in the early years of the nineteenth century. An even closer parallel to the stamp of 1840 was suggested by Charles Knight in 1834. He wanted stamped wrappers to be approved for the tax on newspapers. At that time the law provided that the paper used for newspapers had to be marked with the tax before printing, and this provision materially prevented the improvement in printing processes, as it was impossible to feed continuous rolls into the presses because of this stamping provision. As the newspaper tax did, in effect, provide prepaid postal transmission Knight has as good a claim as anyone to the title of inventor of the postage stamp.

In order to obtain specific ideas, the Treasury opened the field for everybody by announcing a competition on 6 September 1839.

In their pronouncement they mentioned that there were suggestions of stamped covers, stamped paper, and stamps to be used separately. They offered a prize of £200 for the best proposal and £100 for the next best, and they invited entries not only from the people of Britain, but also from foreign countries. There was an element of haste in the whole business, for the entrants had only just over five weeks in which to send in their ideas to Whitehall. The majority of entries suffered from over-ingenuity. But some were extremely close to present-day practice. One entrant, Benjamin Cheverton, proposed printing " a female head of great beauty " or the figure of Mercury embossed on long strips of paper. He experimented with printing them in mile-long strips, and the net cost per stamp, complete with gum, was estimated to work out at $\frac{1}{260}d$. His idea is, of course, basically that used to-day for the rolls of stamps in automatic machines.

A second idea was submitted for a stamp which would serve as a seal and be destroyed when the letter was opened; a third provided a receipt for the sender and another for the postman who was to detach it on delivery. There was another ingenious idea in which geometrical designs indicated the date, and several pointed out that the stamp could be a highly artistic work of cultural value.

One entrant deserves special mention. He was James Chalmers, a Dundee printer. Even to-day there are many people who insist that Chalmers is the real inventor of the postage stamp, and the arguments have for more than a century been quite as heated as those which support the Baconian authorship of Shakespeare's plays. The circumstantial evidence is certainly strong in Chalmers' favour, but against it is the irrefutable fact that Rowland Hill was a man of the very highest integrity. In those developments where he had advice or help he never hesitated to say so, and it is quite out of character that he should deliberately make an exception to this practice in the case of Chalmers, whose entry in the competition received no award. The idea had been also submitted by scores of other entrants by that time.

The real trouble is that Chalmers does not seem to have put forward his idea to the Treasury until the autumn of 1837, some months later than Rowland Hill had himself proposed it. He ran off a few specimens in his printing shop as early as 1834, and he showed these to his friends in the same year. It was, however, rather a nebulous sort of activity of mere academic interest, because at that time all letters were not prepaid, there was no uniform postage, and no one was demanding anything to go on letters beyond the postmark showing distance and place of origin. There was a bigger task ahead than inventing a system of receipt of postage—the organisation of a prepaid system at a standard rate. However, Chalmers' epitaph credits him as the originator of the postage stamp, and some forty years ago a plaque was affixed to his shop in Dundee to the same effect. For ourselves, we are prepared to believe that Rowland Hill improved on the idea of Charles Knight, that he was ignorant of those specimen slips in Dundee when he published his idea for an adhesive stamp, and that it is wholly unjustifiable to suggest that he was guilty of such a petty subterfuge as to steal Chalmers' idea without giving him credit. As a paid Government official at the time of the contest, it would have been quite impossible for him to be awarded a prize, so that even from a financial viewpoint there was no reason for his gainsaying an award to Chalmers if he had merited it.

Some 2,600 entries were submitted for the contest. Rowland Hill solved the problem by announcing four awards of £100 each for the best suggestions, and then took the best proposals, combined them, and called in a firm of Fleet Street printers to discuss the technical side. Henry Cole, the newly appointed assistant to Rowland Hill and one of the winners in the contest just before he obtained the job, was given the task of explaining to the printers what was wanted. They offered to print the stamps at a charge of 8d. per thousand and estimated that they could print 41,600 a day on each press used, starting delivery within a month.

Rowland Hill evidently liked the news that Cole brought him, for the next day he obtained authorisation to engage artists to produce a design. The printers were ordered on 13 December 1839 to prepare a die of Queen Victoria's portrait surrounded by a border and appropriate wording. The Queen's head was to be adapted from a medal struck in honour of the young Queen's visit to the City of London in 1837 which was designed by William Wyon. The pattern round the edge was taken from a standard engine-turned design. After various trial designs and experiments, the final die was ready by the middle of March, and the first sheets of stamps were ready for distribution a month later. These were, of course, the famous Penny Blacks, with check letters appearing in the bottom corners. These letters varied from row to row and were to prevent forgery. The stamps were on sale in London on 1 May, and £2,500 worth were sold on the first day. By 6 May every post office in the country had plentiful supplies—all, that is, except the London sub-post offices. The reason for this exception must have delighted critics of officialdom in those times. A note from the Treasury directed that the issue to the London offices should be delayed. Obediently and unquestioningly, they were held up, though they were on sale at the General Post Office. Rowland Hill, noting that there was this strange vacuum in his stamp sales organisation on 6 May, investigated, and found that some clerk at the Treasury had inscribed the order wrongly. It was intended to read " should *not* be delayed ". The demand for the stamps exceeded all expectations. The printers who suggested quite happily that they could deliver 41,600 daily per machine in their letter of December found that they had to use every press they had and work day and night. They produced more than half a million a day, and were still behind with their orders. The black stamp continued to be printed for the rest of the year, when the colour was changed to red. A total of 283,992 sheets of 240 stamps each was printed, and it is remarkable how comparatively few exist to-day. With specimens fetching £80 from collectors, there must still be many a home with a sizeable windfall tucked away in some old book or pile of yellowing documents which have remained undisturbed for a century or more.

Apart from the adhesive stamps, Rowland Hill provided stamped sheets ready for writing and folding. The design for this stamped cover and envelope was a historic failure. William Mulready, R.A., prepared an illustrative surround which was supposed to be " highly poetic ", but was in fact in execrable taste. The blame for the choice of this artist must rest on the Chancellor of the Exchequer, who told Henry Cole to see Mulready, despite the fact that Cole was already negotiating with a group of artists suggested by the President of the Royal Academy. The design, which was to be printed in the centre of a diamond, the corners of which could then be folded to make an envelope, was a mixture of symbolism and sentimentality, executed with considerable artist's licence. We cannot better the remarks of *The Times* in a description of this remarkable effort:

> We must say that we never beheld anything more ludicrous than the figures or allegorical device by which it is marked with its official character—why not add embellished? Cruikshank could scarcely produce anything so laughable which formed one of the ornaments to Moore's Almanack. Britannia is seated in the centre with the lion couchant (Whig-ish) at her feet; her arms are distended, scattering little flying children to some elephants on the left, and on the right to a group of gentlemen, some of whom at all events are not enclosed in envelopes, writing on their knees, evidently on account of a paucity of tables. There are, besides, sundry figures, who, if they were to appear in the streets of London or on any of our highways, would be liable to penalties of the Vagrant Act for indecent exposure. Under the table-land by which these figures are supported some evidence of laudable curiosity is depicted by three or four ladies who are represented reading a billet doux or Valentine, and some little boys evidently learning to spell, by the mental exertion which their anxious faces disclose.

The design thus described in the " Thunderer's " blast of derision may have been in execrable taste; it was also just about as involved as the space allowed, and the engraving work took more than four months. Even so, the Mulready envelopes were ready by 6 May. *The Times* leaves out any description of the mass of minor detail. There are merchant ships sailing the sea, Red Indians pow-wowing with colonists, camels laden with the goods of the East, men hammering casks. " The Mulreadies " instantly became the Aunt Sally for the witticisms of every lampoonist, entertainer, and caricaturist. The British public, with its healthy instinct for ridiculing the absurd, laughed them out of existence. Within a week Rowland Hill realised they would have to be withdrawn. Great stocks had to be destroyed. Meantime, new envelopes were hurriedly prepared, simply bearing a reproduction of the Queen's head.

It is a remarkable feature of that historic year of 1840 that if the Mulready envelope and cover reached the nadir of stamp artistry, the Penny Black touched the zenith. The lovely portrait of the eighteen-year-old Queen, the bold lettering, the simple background, and the æsthetically satisfying border design have never been improved in all the tens of thousands of British and foreign successors since—the vast majority of which are, of course, imitations of this first stamp.

Queen Victoria herself loved the portrait on the stamp. As the arrangement for the personal selection of stamp designs by the Sovereign was developed, she always insisted that this portrait of herself should be used, and in the long years of her reign the ageing widow of Windsor, the old lady who bewilderedly nodded to the crowds who did homage to her after sixty years on the throne, still appeared on the stamps that travelled to the four corners of her Empire as a young girl thrust by circumstances on the throne of England. No name appeared, no details of the country she ruled; merely the words, " Postage One Penny ". At first there was no need for more, because a stamp could only be British. The tradition remains. A British stamp normally bears the head of the Sovereign, and, with certain unfortunate exceptions, it still has the simple beauty of that first Penny Black. With photogravure printing, dyes and inks which were in 1840 just a chemist's dream, and the greatest artists anxious for the honour of executing the design, that first essay in postage stamp art. hurriedly conceived by a group of officials, artists, and printing craftsmen, can still hold its own against all its successors.

Cancellation of these early stamps was by means of a Maltese cross impression. Postmasters were told how to make up a red ink (" to be well mixed ", said Rowland Hill's recipe), but it did not provide safeguards against erasure by the public. Within a few weeks people were smearing varnish and grease over the stamps so that their friends could wipe off the cancellation marks. Chemists were invited to prepare indelible inks, and other chemists employed to try to get them off. The latter usually managed to do so. Eventually black printer's ink proved most effective, and this was the principle reason why the colour of the stamp itself was changed to red in February 1841.

The next important development was the adoption of an easy method of separating stamps. Henry Archer was the originator of the idea of perforation, and he was invited to send two machines, built at his own expense, to the stamp-printers. They were not a success because of the damage the puncturing points made to the table under the sheets of stamps. The experiments continued with new machines for some years and by 1851 a few sheets of perforated stamps were available. Archer was offered £500 for his idea, and not unnaturally turned it down. Eventually he got £4,000 for the machine, his patent, and his trouble. He had spent £2,000 in making his devices, quite apart from the months of work and experiment. It is remarkable that Rowland Hill, who had himself had experience of the tawdry rewards that the Treasury offered, should have protested that Archer was paid far too much. Later he may have reconsidered his attitude, for he found that the cost of building a machine from the prototype cost the Government £400. There were five of these machines in use in the late fifties.

Although there were many minor changes made in the postage stamps in the years that followed their introduction, most of them concerned such things as watermarks, slight changes in appearance and inks, number of perforations, and so on. They are chiefly of philatelic interest. A more obvious alteration came in 1858, when the code letters appeared in the upper corners as well as in the lower, with a code figure (the sheet number) in the vertical margin. The reason for this was to outwit the more ingenious and dishonest members of the public who had discovered a new method of economising on their postal expenses. It was no longer possible to wash off the postmark without spoiling the stamp, but there was the possibility of matching two used stamps together, using the parts of each which had been missed by the cancelling mark. When suspicions that this was being done resulted in a check on letters passing through London two letters were found, two sections of their stamps so carefully matched that only close examination revealed the joint. Rather ingeniously, an entirely fictitious surcharge of 2s. 6d. was entered on these letters in the hope that they would be refused by the addressees and therefore liable to opening in the Dead Letter Office, where the identity of the sender would enable prosecution to follow. But the heavy payments were met, presumably because the recipients realised what the Post Office was up to.

If no example of punishment could be made, rearrangement of the check letters could be adopted to make the fraud virtually impossible. The letters would have to match the code and the figures in the vertical margins be identical. Except by luck or literally months of searching, no one could find the right halves to stick together, a form of employment hardly rewarded by the saving of 1*d*.

By 1844 the maltese cross cancellation mark had been changed to a code number for each town, and shortly afterwards the place and date stamp, which was still being used in addition to the stamp cancellation mark, was combined with the code number. The postmark as we know it to-day was not adopted until 1895, though the circle (without the time of posting) had come into use ten years earlier.

The London printers (Perkins, Bacon, and Petch) who had quoted their price for the stamp printings cannot have visualised the huge job they were undertaking. They had contracts for five-year periods, and they reduced the price for printing in July 1851 to 5*d*. per thousand. In the following year the need for a 4*d*. stamp for posts to France brought acceptable quotations from the firm of Thomas De La Rue, who had successfully experimented with the use of electrotype plates for surface printing. The new stamps were carmine in colour, printed on a blue-tinted paper. They were on sale to the public in July 1855. Two years later 6*d*. stamps in lilac and 1*s*. stamps in dark green were issued. New values quickly followed—a 4*d*. dark red and a 9*d*. bistre in 1862, and a few months later a 3*d*. carmine rose-red. Higher values— from 2*s*. up to £5—appeared at intervals up to 1878. A year later, the line-engraved process used from 1840 on the 1*d*. stamps was abandoned. The new penny stamps (which were printed by De La Rue) went on sale on New Year's Day, 1880. They were clean and clear, but they lacked the richness of the older stamps. Although the original printers had quoted for the new 1*d*. stamp contracts as well as for the new $\frac{1}{2}d.$, $1\frac{1}{2}d.$, and $2d.$ stamps required, they were unsuccessful, and the forty years of never-ceasing printing work that Perkins, Bacon, and Petch had carried out finally came to an end.

To-day our postage stamps up to and including $1s.$ in value bear the words "Postage Revenue". The distinction between postage and revenue stamps was abolished in 1882 by Act of Parliament. A new $1d.$ stamp, lilac in colour, anticipated the Act by including both these words, and all lower values were so printed by 1884. The stamps of the Victorian era created much work in the investigation of inks, papers, and printing processes, but it was not until 1901 that the problem of a new design arose with the Accession of Edward VII.

The portrait and the frame design of the new stamp were the work of an Austrian sculptor, Emil Fuchs, and were personally selected by the King. Photography was used to obtain the original. The sketch and the design for the border were photographed separately and a third plate made of the two superimposed. The first Edward VII stamps ($\frac{1}{2}d.$, $1d.$, $2\frac{1}{2}d.$, and $6d.$) were on sale by 1 January 1902. No one seems to have liked them, though the criticisms were directed against the artist more than against his work. The attitude of Germany and her friends during the Boer War and the growing sense of foreboding about the future activities of the Central European Powers made it a somewhat unwise move to have used an Austrian for work of national importance. However, the basic designs remained for Edward VII's short reign, though there were many experiments in colour changes, principally to avoid confusion under artificial light. The $1d.$ lilac was probably the most notable of these. It returned to red. One curious little anecdote of the Edwardian stamps bears re-telling. One of the last values planned was a $7d.$ stamp. It appeared on 4 May 1910, a greyish-black effort which gave the impression of a mourning stamp. The whole country knew that the King had by then become suddenly ill, and two days after the stamp was first put on sale he died.

The unexpected death of the Sovereign aggravated the difficulties of the contract for stamp-printing, which was just then being moved from De La Rue to Harrison & Sons. The latter firm were very old-established printers for the Government, but the processing of stamps was an entirely new field for them. There was not sufficient time to prepare designs bearing the portrait of George V, and when Harrisons started operations on 1 January 1911, they continued with the Edwardian stamps for low values (the Board of Inland Revenue undertaking the work of printing the remainder at Somerset House) until the new plates were ready.

There was already a precedent for an outcry about a new design for postage stamps. To-day, of course, it is so routine that the Post Office officials would doubtless be worried if it did not occur, but on Coronation Day, 22 June 1911, when the first of the new stamps appeared, there was an outcry which must have given cynical amusement to the ghost of William Mulready, designer of the ill-starred envelope of 1840. Plans were put in hand on 1 July 1910, when the Postmaster-General, Mr. Herbert Samuel, asked several artists to submit designs. They were to include a lion couchant. None was of any use, and Sir Bertram MacKennal, who had designed the new coinage, was invited to design the new stamp.

King George V was anxious that the stamp should bear a true likeness rather than an idealised impression, and so a photograph was used. Sir Bertram designed the frame, and a heraldic artist, G. W. Eve, was responsible for the lettering. From the first meeting until the public sale of the stamps (only the $\frac{1}{2}d.$ and 1$d.$ values were ready by Coronation Day), art work, production and printing had taken nearly eleven months. Everybody hastened to say that the time had been ill-spent. No one had a good word to say for them. There were questions in Parliament and the Postmaster-General promised that " steps would be taken ". The steps did little to improve things except to the expert eye of the technician, but by August 1912 the first of a new series, with the head of the King drawn from the relief modelling used on the coinage, made its appearance. The lion had disappeared, the frame was improved and everybody felt much happier. By 1913 the first George V issues were all replaced. Then came the Great War, and there were bigger problems for Parliament, press and people to face. With minor changes, the stamps that were on general sale in 1913 continued until the end of the reign—in the case of some high values until 1939.

Some small countries materially assist their overseas revenue by the regular issue of special stamps, which have an immediate export value among philatelists. No country in the world is as wary of stunts of this kind as the United Kingdom. Only the death of the Sovereign used to bring any major change, and even now an event has to be of truly historic or postal importance to merit a commemorative issue: Queen Victoria's Jubilees, the end of the Boer War, the Armistice of 1918—all passed without postal notice. The first occasion for a special stamp came with the British Empire Exhibition at Wembley in 1924. The stamps were produced in 1d. and 1½d. values and were sold only at the Exhibition. Sir G. E. P. Murrary, Secretary to the Post Office, headed the committee which selected the suitable design, the work of Harold Nelson. The King's head was the original from the stamps of 1913 and the lion was drawn from the rather modernistic animal which was the emblem of the Exhibition.

When the Postal Union met in London in 1929 the Post Office was faced with the fact that by tradition the delegates were always presented with a set of stamps of the host in commemoration of the occasion. The idea was to restrict the issue to the four low values, ½d., 1d., 1½d., and 2½d.—until someone pointed out that this would mean presenting the members of the Congress with a gift of face value 5½d. For the sake of prestige, a £1 value was added. The latter was a magnificent stamp bearing the coinage head of the King, the words " Postal Union Congress London 1929 " and a portrayal of St. George and the dragon. It was, as a matter of interest, an adaptation of one of Harold Nelson's designs for the Wembley Exhibition Stamp.

At the time of the Silver Jubilee of George V in 1935 the Post Office was in the midst of a heavy publicity campaign run by Sir Kingsley Wood. Public relations had become an important department of the Post Office. Better pens, brighter post offices, slogans to make the public write more, telegraph more, and telephone often brought something entirely unfamiliar into the running of a Government department. Whether this policy was also responsible for the decision to issue Jubilee stamps is, of course, a matter of opinion; certainly it broke all precedent. The four popular values were issued, and once more the coinage head was used. The desired effect was of dignity and simplicity, and in this the artist, Barnett Freedman, admirably succeeded.

A year before the Silver Jubilee the first photogravure stamps were issued. They brought certain modifications of colour and design because of the new process, but in general the change was for the better.

Stamps for the short reign of Edward VIII were produced in less than eight months after he came to the throne. This time the Post Office was very cautious and announced that the designs were being issued tentatively to obtain the public's reaction. This wariness was readily understandable, for the design was puritanically austere. The Hugh Cecil portrait photograph appeared on a plain background. The only word, apart from the value, which appeared was " Postage ", and there was no frame. Considering how unconventional the stamp was, it had a very good reception, the chief critics being the artistic fraternity, who felt chagrined at the use of what was virtually a plain photograph. The pleasing appearance, however, was due as much as anything to this ideal medium for photogravure. If these stamps had had longer life they would probably have set an entirely new style for stamps generally. But by the turn of events they were replaced by May 1937 with the hurriedly produced stamps of George VI. This included a special Coronation 1½d. issue. Edmond Dulac was the artist responsible for this symbolic yet accurate design. It was deservedly popular. Even better from an æsthetic viewpoint were the George VI general issues. Here Dulac's fine head was enhanced by the lettering and design of Eric Gill. The combination of a great watercolour artist with one of the generation's leading typographers and sculptors produced a stamp design which was a pleasing compromise between the George V ornateness and the Edward VIII austerity. Edmond Dulac brilliantly captured the formal tone set by the original postage stamp without losing the photographic veracity which is the great feature of photogravure reproduction.

Of the recent commemorative issues it is not necessary to make more than passing reference. There was the Centenary issue of

One of the most famous of the Cunard mail steamers: the original " Mauretania ", which maintained the Old-New World service between 1907 and 1934.

TOP: The first United Kingdom aerial post—between Hendon and Windsor—i[n] 1911.   BOTTOM: An historic airgraph letter, the 100 millionth, sent by Genera[l] Eisenhower.

The original letters, written on standard Airgraph forms, passing through the Post Office sorting department before photography.

May 1940, planned to coincide with a big exhibition to be held in London. Although the outbreak of war at first brought a decision to abandon the issue, the Post Office eventually went ahead, and the stamps were on sale on 6 May 1940. A strange contrast it was indeed with the same day a hundred years before. Then Britain was in the third decade of what was to be nearly a century of peace. Now the Panzer divisions were sweeping across the Low Countries, and France was soon to be overwhelmed.

This Centenary stamp, which many people hardly noticed on their letters in the excitement of those days, showed the original head of Victoria beside the head of George VI. The only indication of the reason for the issue was " 1840-1940 ". Many people, even in Britain, were unaware what these dates stood for, and still more overseas correspondents were quite ignorant of their significance.

If France had not capitulated at this time there would have been a really epoch-making stamp in our albums to-day. This was to be two Anglo-French stamps of similar design but issued only in the country of use, printed in blue and marked " 1 fr. 50 " and " $2\frac{1}{2}d$." It was scheduled to appear in October 1940, but, of course, all the plans for this notable international occasion had to be abandoned with the temporary defeat of our ally.

Since the war there have been the Silver Wedding stamps (the £1 stamp being the first since the withdrawal of this value in 1937), the Channel Islands Liberation issue and the Olympic Games stamp. The quick succession of these commemoratives would seem to indicate that the rigid policy of the first years of British postage stamps has now been relaxed, and there is really no reason why this should not be so.

Printing and production of modern postage stamps is as fine an example of the craftsman's art as one can find. It is a long and intricate process in which human skill is allied to uncanny technical developments. The original stamp design is photographed, after which the negative is carefully retouched. From this master negative a step-and-repeat camera produces on glass 480 positive images of the stamp. Between each exposure an adjustment is made to ensure accurate positioning of each image, and after all

10

the images have been photographed, cylinder numbers and control marks are added. The positive images on the sheet are then ready for transfer to the printing cylinder. This is achieved by carbon tissue, which is a heavy paper coated with a layer of gelatine. The tissue is made sensitive to light by immersion in a solution of bichromate, dried, and then pressed in contact with a screen.

The screen is an opaque sheet of glass with a network of lines numbering 150-200 to the inch in each direction. This screen allows light to pass through the clear lines and causes the sensitised tissue to harden. Next the positive, with its 480 images of the stamp, is placed in contact with the tissue and exposed. The light passes through to the tissue in proportion to the tone values of the positive, and the tissue is now ready for transfer to the printing cylinder, which is of copper-plated steel.

The paper base of the tissue is removed by hot water, so that only sensitised gelatine remains, the unsensitised portions, which do not harden, are also washed away. Areas not to be etched—the divisions between the stamps, edges, etc.—are painted with acid-resisting paint, and then the actual etching process, taking between fifteen and thirty minutes, begins. A solution of ferric chloride, which only penetrates gelatine when diluted with water, eats into the tissue skin, reaching the copper printing surface of the cylinder through the small cells formed by the screen, thus penetrating the metal surface in proportion to the strength of the positive tone. The moment when the acid has done its work is decided by the operator, and only experience will decide when that moment has come.

Proofs are taken so that the fine etcher, who now takes over, can start eradicating minor imperfections by hand. This is, of course, a work of delicate artistry, and takes many hours of pains-taking examination and brush-work. After further inspection, the cylinder is passed for printing.

Before the paper can be fed into the machines it has to be gummed. Gum arabic is used, and despite the scares started a century ago, it is absolutely harmless, and is subject to rigorous chemical tests so that the busiest stamp-licking office-boy will never come to any harm from a diet of the " glutinous wash ". To restrict frothing when the solution is spread on the stamp paper, pure milk is added, the only ingredient which is suitable under the Pure Food laws. After gumming, the continuous reels of paper are hung to allow them to dry in a uniform temperature and humidity.

Highly volatile ink is used on the rotary presses, and the drying process is further speeded up by hot-air blowers. There is, of course, some wastage from the machines at the beginning and end of the run, and all such sheets have to be carefully accounted for. At every stage proofs, imperfect stamps, and errors are collected and reassembled in sheets so that, with the completed sheets of perfect stamps, they will tally with the original supply of paper. Stamp-collectors who know the great sums which are paid for examples of errors in postage stamp printing or perforation will realise how rarely does this careful checking fail. Harrison & Sons Ltd., who produce up to 30 millions of British postage stamps daily, are justly proud that no country in the world can show so few rarities.

Milestones in Post Office History

1482. Relays of messengers organised to carry Royal despatches.

1516. Sir Brian Tuke appointed Master of the King's Posts.

1545. Office of Master of the Messengers, Runners, and Posts created.

1566. Thomas Randolph appointed Master of the Posts.

1583. Rules for the Inland Posts laid down.

1591. Proclamation prohibiting unofficial Overseas Posts.

1598. Fixed Posts on main roads set up.

1619. The de Questers appointed Postmasters for Foreign Parts.

1632. Orders for day and night postal facilities between London and Dover.

1635. Proclamation for the Settling of the Letter Offices of England and Scotland.

1650. Franking privilege begins.

1653. John Manley, first Postmaster under the farming system, takes office.

1657. Cromwell's Statute regularises the postal service for the British Isles.

1660. The Post Office Charter.

1669. Posts on by-roads.

1680. Dockwra Penny Post in London.

1682. Dockwra system taken over by the Post Office.

1711. Act to unify the Post Office in the British Isles.

1720. Cross-Posts inaugurated.

1764. Authority to set up local Penny Posts in provincial towns
        obtained.

1765. More reasonable rates for overseas letters.

1773. General Turnpike Act allows road improvements.

1784. First mail coach runs from Bristol to London.

1792. Money Order Office opened.

1797-1801-1805-1812. General increases of postage rates during
        Napoleonic Wars.

1830. Mails go by railway for the first time between Manchester
        and Liverpool.

1837. Admiralty takes over organisation of mail packets.
        Constitution of the Post Office regularised.
        Overland mail service to India.
        Rowland Hill's pamphlet on Postal Reform published.

1838. First travelling post office.

1839. Treasury empowered to prescribe rates by warrant.
        Registration introduced.

1840. Uniform Penny Postage.
        First issue of postage stamps.
        Franking ceases.

1841. Embossed envelopes issued.

1859. First limited mail train runs.

1860. Admiralty control of mail packets relinquished.

1861. Post Office Savings Bank Act passed.

1864. Post Office insurance policies and annuities on sale.

1866. Meetings of Post Office employees forbidden.

1870.   Post Office takes over telegraph services.
        Postcards introduced.

1871.   New scales of postage.

1874.   Universal Postal Union Act signed in Switzerland.

1876.   Telephone introduced into Great Britain.

1881.   Postal orders introduced.

1882.   Reply postcards issued.

1884.   Parcels post.

1885.   Reduced postal charges on heavy letters.
        Special mail train between London and Aberdeen.

1889.   Telegraph money order system started as experiment.

1890.   Postmen's Strike.
        Celebrations on Jubilee of Penny Post.

1891.   Postmen's Federation formed.
        Railway letter service started.

1892.   Letter cards introduced.

1895.   Wireless telegraphy link established between Crookhaven
        Post Office and Fastnet Lighthouse.

1896.   Tweedmouth Committee improves employees' conditions.

1897.   Victoria's Diamond Jubilee concessions: reduced rates;
        delivery to every home in the country.

1898.   Motor vans first used.

1899.   Uniform scale of postage rates on parcels for a large part
        of the Commonwealth.

1902.   First G.P.O. telephone exchange (Central) opened.

1904-7. Bradford and Hobhouse Committees improve administra-
        tion and employee conditions.

1905.   Official parcels post to U.S.A.

1906. Inland parcels post rates reduced.

1908. Overseas C.O.D. system started.

1911. First official air mail between Hendon and Windsor.

1918. Penny postage letter rate abandoned.

1920. Union of Post Office Workers formed.
       Whitley Councils.

1927. Post Office underground railway opened.

1932. Bridgeman Committee advises decentralisation of control.

1940. Centenary of the Penny Post celebrations.

1949. Helicopters used experimentally for rural posts.

The Office of Postmaster-General

Under the Acts of 1657 and 1660 the activities of the Post Office were defined by law, with a Postmaster-General in charge, appointed either for life or a period of ten years, the sum paid annually for the privilege being decided (after 1660) by the monarch. The first holder, Henry Bishop, was granted the position in farm at a yearly rental of £21,500. He disposed of it in 1663 to Daniel O'Neile, who died in October 1664, and the position was then nominally held by his widow, Katherine, Countess of Chesterfield. She died in 1667.

From that date until 1823 the Post Office management was usually shared between two Postmasters-General. At first one was the active partner, and it was the practice to appoint a deputy, who in fact carried out the major part of the executive work. Then, in 1689, the two appointments were normally allocated on a political basis—one to a Whig and the other to a Tory. Where these deputies are notable from a historical viewpoint their names are given in the following list.

LORD ARLINGTON *(Deputy, Sir John Bennett)* ⎫
⎬ 1667.
LORD BERKELEY *(Deputy, Andrew Ellis)* ⎭
(Sir John Bennett left in 1672 and Andrew Ellis died a month later. Roger Whitley then became sole Deputy.)

EARL OF ROCHESTER   -   -   -   - 1677.
(Sir Philip Frowde was also appointed at this time and was known as the Governor of the Post Office.)

MAJOR JOHN WILDMAN   -   -   -   - 1689.

Sir Robert Cotton
Sir Thomas Frankland } - - - 1691.

Sir Thomas Frankland
Sir John Evelyn } - - - 1708.

Lord Cornwallis
James Craggs } - - - 1715.

Edward Carteret
Galfridus Walpole } - - - 1720.

Edward Carteret
Edward Harrison } - - - 1725.

Edward Carteret - - - - 1732.

Edward Carteret
Lord Lovel } - - 1733.

Lord Lovel
Sir John Eyles } - - - 1739.

Earl of Leicester *(Lord Lovel)* - - 1744.

Earl of Leicester
Sir Everard Fawkener } - - - 1745.

Earl of Leicester - - - 1758.

Earl of Bessborough
Robert Hampden } - - - 1759.

Earl of Egmont
Robert Hampden } - - - 1762.

Lord Hyde
Robert Hampden } - - - 1763.

Earl of Bessborough
Lord Grantham } - - - 1765.

Earl of Hillsborough
Lord Le Despencer } - - - 1766.

EARL OF SANDWICH ⎱
LORD LE DESPENCER ⎰ - - - - 1768.

LORD LE DESPENCER ⎱
H. F. THYNNE *(afterwards Carteret)* ⎰ - 1771.

H. F. CARTERET *(formerly Thynne)* - - 1781.

VISCOUNT BARRINGTON ⎱
H. F. CARTERET ⎰ - - - - - 1782.

EARL OF TANKERVILLE ⎱
H. F. CARTERET ⎰ - - - - 1782.

LORD FOLEY ⎱
H. F. CARTERET ⎰ - - - - - 1783.

H. F. CARTERET *(later Lord Carteret)* - 1784.

EARL OF CLAREDON ⎱
LORD CARTERET ⎰ - - - - 1786.

LORD CARTERET ⎱
LORD WALSINGHAM ⎰ - - - - 1787.

LORD WALSINGHAM ⎱
EARL OF WESTMORLAND ⎰ - - - - 1789.

LORD WALSINGHAM ⎱
EARL OF CHESTERFIELD ⎰ - - - - 1790.

EARL OF CHESTERFIELD ⎱
EARL OF LEICESTER ⎰ - - - - 1794.

EARL OF LEICESTER ⎱
LORD AUCKLAND ⎰ - - - - 1798.

LORD AUCKLAND ⎱
LORD GOWER ⎰ - - - - 1799.

LORD AUCKLAND ⎱
LORD C. SPENCER ⎰ - - - - 1801.

LORD C. SPENCER }
DUKE OF MONTROSE } - - - - **1804.**

EARL OF BUCKINGHAMSHIRE }
EARL OF CARYSFOOT } - - - **1806.**

EARL OF SANDWICH }
EARL OF CHICHESTER } - - - - **1807.**

EARL OF CHICHESTER - - - - **1814.**

EARL OF CHICHESTER }
EARL OF CLANCARTY } - - - - **1814.**

EARL OF CHICHESTER }
MARQUESS OF SALISBURY } - - - **1816.**

EARL OF CHICHESTER - - - - **1823.**

LORD FREDERICK MONTAGUE - - - **1826.**

DUKE OF MANCHESTER - - - - **1827.**

DUKE OF RICHMOND - - - - **1830.**
(*By his first Patent, Postmaster-General of Great Britain; by a second, dated 14 April 1831, Postmaster-General of Great Britain and Ireland.*)

MARQUESS OF CONYNGHAM - - - **1834.**

LORD MARYBOROUGH - - - - **1834.**

MARQUESS OF CONYNGHAM - - - **1835**

EARL OF LICHFIELD - - - - **1835.**

LORD LOWTHER (*afterwards Earl of Lonsdale*) - - - - - - **1841.**

EARL OF ST. GERMAN'S - - - - **1846.**

MARQUESS OF CLANRICARDE - - - **1846.**

EARL OF HARDWICK - - - - **1852.**

VISCOUNT CANNING - - - - **1853.**

DUKE OF ARGYLE - - - - - **1855**

LORD COLCHESTER - - - - -	1858.
EARL OF ELGIN - - - - -	1859.
DUKE OF ARGYLE · - - - -	1860.
LORD STANLEY OF ALDERLEY - - -	1860.
DUKE OF MONTROSE - - - -	1866.
MARQUESS OF HARTINGTON - - -	1868.
WM. MONSELL - - - - -	1871.
LYON PLAYFAIR *(later Lord Playfair)* -	1873.
LORD JOHN MANNERS - - - -	1874.
HENRY FAWCETT - - - - -	1880.
GEORGE J. S. LEFEVRE - - - -	1884.
LORD JOHN MANNERS - - - -	1885.
LORD WOLVERTON - - - - -	1886.
H. CECIL RAIKES - - - - -	1886.
SIR J. FERGUSSON - - - - -	1891.
ARNOLD MORLEY - - - - -	1892.
DUKE OF NORFOLK - - - - -	1895
MARQUESS OF LONDONDERRY - - -	1900.
J. AUSTEN CHAMBERLAIN - - -	1902.
LORD STANLEY - - - - -	1903.
SIDNEY BUXTON - - - - -	1905.
HERBERT SAMUEL - - - - -	1910.
C. E. H. HOBHOUSE - - - -	1914.
HERBERT SAMUEL *(later Viscount Samuel)*	1915.
J. A. PEASE *(later Lord Gainford)* - -	1916.
A. H. ILLINGWORTH *(later Lord Illing-worth)* - - - - - -	1916.
F. G. KELLAWAY - - - - -	1921.
NEVILLE CHAMBERLAIN - - - -	1922.

Sir William Joynson-Hicks *(later Viscount Brentford)* - - - - 1923.

Sir Laming Worthington Evans - - 1923.

Vernon Hartshorn - - - - 1924.

Sir William Mitchell-Thomson *(later Lord Selsdon)* - - - - - 1924.

H. B. Lees-Smith - - - - 1929.

C. R. Attlee - - - - - 1931.

W. A. Ormsby-Gore *(later Lord Harlech)* 1931.

Sir Kingsley Wood - - - - 1931.

G. C. Tryon *(later Lord Tryon)* - - 1935.

W. S. Morrison - - - - - 1940.

Captain H. F. C. Crookshank - - 1943.

Earl of Listowel - - - - - 1945.

Wilfred Paling - - - - - 1947.

Ness Edwards - - - - - 1950.

Bibliography

Autobiography. ANTHONY TROLLOPE.

British Almanac. (1828 onwards.)

British Merchant Adventurers. MAURICE COLLIS. (1942.)

British Post Office, The. HOWARD ROBINSON (U.S.A. publication). (1947.)

Carriages and Coaches. R. STRAUS. (1912.)

Civil Air Transport. GROUP CAPTAIN W. E. WYNN. (1945.)

Elizabethan Journals. G. B. HARRISON. (1928.)

English Inn, The. THOMAS BURKE. (1947.)

Forty Years at the Post Office. F. E. BAINES. (1898.)

From Post Boy to Air Mail. G. GIBBARD JACKSON. (——).

From Track to By-pass. T. WILKINSON. (1934.)

Gibbons' Stamp Monthly.

G.P.O. E. T. CRUTCHLEY. (1938.)

Haste, Post, Haste! GEORGE WALKER. (1938.)

History of British Postage Stamps. T. TODD. (1941.)

History of British Postmarks. J. H. DANIELS. (1898.)

History of the G.W.R. E. T. MACDERMOT. (1927.)

History of the Homeland. HENRY HAMILTON. (1947.)

Hundred-year History of the P. & O., The. BOYD CABLE. (1937.)

Life and Work of the Peoples of England: Fourteenth, Fifteenth, Sixteenth and Seventeenth Centuries. DOROTHY HARTLEY and MARGARET M. ELLIOT. (1925-31.)

Life of Sir Francis Drake. A. E. W. MASON. (1941.)

Life of Sir Rowland Hill. G. B. HILL. (1880.)

Paston Letters, The. Edited by J. GAIRDNER. (1904.)

Philatelic Magazine.

Post, The. Organ of the Union of Post Office Workers.

Post Annual.

Post Office, The: An Historical Summary. Official publication. (1911.)

Post Office Commercial Accounts. Official. (Annually.)

Post Office Reform. VISCOUNT WOLMER. (1932.)

Post Office Went to War, The. IAN HAY. Official. (1946.)

Report on Financial Assistance to Civil Air Transport Companies. Official. (1923.)

Revenue Departments' Appropriation Accounts. Official. (Annually.)

Selections from the Journals and Papers of John Byrom. Edited by HENRI TALON. (Rockliff, 1951.)

Stamp Collecting. STANLEY PHILLIPS. (6th edn., 1946.)

Stamp Magazine.

Story of the Road. J. W. GREGORY. (1931.)

World's Airways, The. (1950.)

INDEX